"When I think of the quest t
capital punishment, Jeff Hoo
come to mind. This book creatively and passionately puts
forward a case that I hope all Christians will listen to."
— Benjamin L. Corey, author of *Undiluted: Rediscovering the
Radical Message of Jesus*

"Jeff Hood has the blisters that come from a journey such as
this. He asks the questions hardest to answer for Christians who
root their support for executions in the Bible. Via mileposts
like Helen Prejean, Karla Faye Tucker, Troy Davis, and Kelly
Gissendaner on roads in Texas, Georgia, Ohio, and elsewhere, we
get answers. He walks with Jesus. Read this book."
— Abraham J. Bonowitz, DeathPenaltyAction.org

"Jeff Hood is in the vanguard of a new spirituality for a new
age."
— Stephen V. Sprinkle, Brite Divinity School at Texas
Christian University

"Here, for devout Christians whose interpretation of their faith
allows the embrace of state killing, are some thoughts for their
consideration. Rev. Dr. Jeff Hood, a committed Baptist minister
from the South, offers some meditations on *The Execution of
God*."
— Mike Farrell, actor ("M*A*S*H") and President of Death
Penalty Focus

"Jeff Hood is one of the nation's leading voices against the death
penalty. In this work, he shows us that in our common bloodlust
to kill the Other, we put ourselves at risk of killing God."
— Anthony Grimes, Fellowship of Reconciliation

"*The Execution of God* is a revelation. Rev. Hood's lone fist of
resistance evolved into a movement to truly love your neighbor
as yourself and examine our own Christianity. Never stop
walking, Jeff."
— Brian Stolarz, attorney and friend to death row exoneree
and author of *Grace and Justice on Death Row*

"After reading *The Execution of God,* I have many questions racing through my mind. If we are made in the image of God, what if God is not all about killing God's self? What would it look like if manhood were not correlated to violence? If killers get to repent before their execution, when does our society get to repent of our sin of murder? For those of us in the restorative justice movement, or those of us whose hearts cannot break into any more fragments over the violence unnecessarily part of our justice system, this book is poetry—not to soothe the soul but to awaken it."

— Sandhya Jha, Oakland Peace Center

"Jeff Hood's Sunday school teacher taught him that 'God invented the death penalty.' This book serves as a lesson in how to how unlearn that teaching, and helps us understand that, instead, 'God feels the needle.' It's the story of Jeff Hood's engagement, his walking pilgrimages to death row, and his friendships with people who took lives. *The Execution of God* is full of questions that lead us to ponder several books' worth of answers – and maybe start living abolition in our lives. May this book be shared throughout congregations as an example of how each of us, particularly those who identify as Christian, must unbind each other from our addiction to death."

— Steve Dear, People of Faith Against the Death Penalty

"Jeff Hood's passionate work against the death penalty leaves no doubt that abolition is imminent."

— Jason Redick, Holy Covenant UMC in Carrolton, Texas

"The prophetic voice of Rev. Jeff Hood calls out to his fellow Christians to acknowledge the dissonance of worshiping a legally executed (crucified) Lord and supporting a system that kills under color of justice. May all be moved to remove from our hearts the thirst for vengeance!"

— Ven. Tashi Nyima, Nying Je Ling, Universal Compassion Buddhist Congregation, Dallas

"Jeff Hood raises critical questions that have long concerned those of us in the field of faith-based social activism against the death penalty. Do you consider the execution of God? How do we point to the death penalty's theological and legalistic contradictions in ways that accurately capture the complexities as well as speak to a broad audience of policy makers, government administrators, and people on both sides of this issue? And, what should we do with the results of such assessments as flawed human beings? Jeff's book *The Execution of God* is also for cynics, conservatives, and pro-death penalty people. His voice is raw and honest enough to make believers out of anybody."
   — Nikki Roberts, author of *Freed From Within*

"Dr. Hood walked 30 miles for abolition with a group in Ohio. From death row to the statehouse, Hood never stopped crying out for the abolition of the abomination that is the death penalty. In all of his actions, Dr. Hood is in touch with the best of the prophetic tradition. If you lend your eyes to this book, your heart will follow."
   — Sam R. Sheppard, son of Dr. Sam Sheppard, wrongfully convicted of murder in Ohio in 1954

"In *The Execution of God*, Jeff Hood shepherds the reader on a dark, meandering path of stories about death and life. As with his other books, Hood asks aloud what some are afraid to think; he provokes readers to consider 'Would a loving God kill?' while daring us to glimpse a frighteningly dynamic divine, one that is bloodthirsty yet compassionate, breathtaking yet breathgiving. Hood reflects profoundly on his own experiences with the children of God meted to suffer the capital punishment; these stories are tormenting and intimate. His testimony and questions advance a radical, revolutionary, and avant-garde theology of love. I highly recommend."
   — Jason Smith, congregational consultant

"Rev. Dr. Jeff Hood is a giant amongst abolitionists."
   — Will Speer, Texas death row

"By turns Hemingwayesque, cinematic *a la* Sartre, and thoroughly stream-of-consciousness, Jeff Hood's book explores what it means for each of us to be made in the image of God. Does it mean that divinity meets divinity even in the midst of a crime, perpetrator and victim? God is in prison. God is condemned to die. God lives on death row. God is led to the chamber. God is strapped to the gurney. We only kill each other by denying God in the other. Yet following God is about celebrating life. If it ain't love, it ain't God."
— Max Hess, attorney

"Jeff Hood's *The Execution of God* is both a testament of personal transformation and a work of profound theological study. He asks the hard questions no one else has dared to ask for fear the answers would shatter their faith. Instead, the answers don't shatter faith, but rather strengthen the very core of why we believe. The text challenges us to sift the chaff from the wheat in our held doctrines to discover the essence of a loving God who calls us to love our neighbors as ourselves, not kill them."
— Fred L Hammond, Unitarian Universalist Congregation of Tuscaloosa

"Jeff Hood's work has deepened my commitment to liberation theology."
— Jim Mitulski, Metropolitan Community Church, United Church of Christ and Disciples of Christ

"Jeff Hood always reminds us that theology is based in story."
— Mike Wright-Chapman, funeral director

"There are few voices in the Christian world like that of Rev. Dr. Jeff Hood."
— Ray Jordan, Central Congregational United Church of Christ, Dallas

"Jeff Hood continues to press us into an ever-expanding gallery of inclusive images of God."
— Imam La Trina Jackson, Muslims for Progressive Values

"Jeff Hood is an extraordinary theologian who uses precision mixed with creativity to elevate the theological discourse. Hood's determination to intersect theology and praxis through activism demands our attention to his prophetic voice."
— Mitchell Boone, White Rock United Methodist Church, Dallas

"Let Jeff Hood take you beyond language to the mind of God."
— Andrew Robinson, Young Progressive Christians of Dallas

"I have come to depend on Jeff Hood to help me think about matters of theology in a fresh, imaginative, and insightful way. I am exceedingly grateful for his passion."
— Lee Ann Bryce, First Congregational United Church of Christ, Fort Worth

"Personal and Scriptural, reason-filled and spirit-filled, *The Execution of God* takes aim at not only the idea of the death penalty, but what each one of us needs to do to eradicate this antichristian practice. Rev. Dr. Jeff Hood challenged me to get off my seat, out of my house, and join the resistance toward ending the death penalty!"
— Kyle Tubbs, Peace of Christ Church, Round Rock, Texas

"There are rare leaders that pop up in the world of religion. In a time when clergy are silent and inactive about injustice, Jeff Hood has the courage to step up and speak out against the death penalty. This book highlights a path toward becoming one of the lead authorities on the subject...I highly recommend it."
— Ashton Woods, atheist Southerner and founder/lead organizer of Black Lives Matter: Houston

"Dr. Jeff Hood is God's man in the fight against the death penalty. Bringing light to darkness, Dr. Hood is a prophet for the condemned. Salvation is found in these pages."
— Olinka Green, Community Prophet, Dallas

"Texas is trying to kill my husband. Juan Balderas is innocent. As the wife of this condemned man, I know the power of Jeff Hood's work. We have repeatedly stood together for abolition. The mysticism that Jeff brings to our work is strange and impactful. Repeatedly, Jeff has shouted down the powerful and demanded justice. Because of his work, numerous families have been given voice as their loved ones are marched to the death chamber. Hear his words. You will be changed. #FreeJuanBalderas"
— Yancy Balderas, Abolitionist

"Throughout this misguided state, Jeff Hood loudly proclaims the truth of Jesus—'God and killing just don't mix.'"
— Father Fred Clarkson, Episcopal Diocese of Texas

"Captive to their reckless love for the condemned, I hear God and Jeff Hood screaming the same thing, 'F--- the death penalty.'"
— Dan Kiniry, Pilgrims in the Park

"I've walked many miles with Jeff Hood. I encourage you to open this book and walk a few miles too."
— Mike McCleese, Queer Abolitionist

"With apocalyptic and poetic artistry, Jeff Hood makes a case for love, rooted in thoughtful and provocative biblical exegesis, that abolishes the death penalty once and for all. Readers like myself may never think the same again about our Christian faith and its potential to embrace the condemned as we see in them the God we hope to know in ourselves."
— Brian Henderson, First Baptist Church of Denver

"Jeff Hood is a modern day incarnational reminder that Jesus has always called us to be revolutionary assholes that change the world."
— John Holbrook, Abolitionist

"Jeff Hood is a death penalty abolitionist, impassioned and earthy, challenging the practice in light of a relentless theology of radical grace and radical justice. His book is a 'hard saying' from start to finish, compelling us to confront the implications and depth of *imago dei* in human beings and the society in which we live."
— Bill J. Leonard, Wake Forest University School of Divinity

"There's an old Jewish proverb that says, 'Before every person there marches an angel proclaiming, "Behold, the image of God."' Jeff Hood is that angel proclaiming before every death penalty inmate that they have value. May we pay attention to his prophetic voice in order to stop the execution of God's people."
— Danny Cortez, New Heart Community Church, Whittier, California

"This is another prophetic work by one of the most prolific and original theologians of my generation, Dr. Jeff Hood. This book trains the theological eye on the death penalty, using fresh language to shine a light on a moral failure which Christians have turned away from since Christ himself was executed. This is an important piece for both conservative Christians who consider themselves pro-life and progressive Christians who consider themselves champions of social justice."
— Anna Humble, pastor

"Jeff Hood and I met while visiting prisoners on death row. Jeff embraces with open arms the 'other,' the condemned, the marginalized, the poor, teaching us all that difference between 'us and them' is a fiction we should let go. I've never known anyone so fully committed to ending the death penalty in the United States or who puts his body so fully where his heart is. Read this book and you will understand on many levels why the death penalty is killing us all."
— Dani Clark, the Community of Sant'Egidio

"Jeff Hood's *The Execution of God: Encountering the Death Penalty* is a powerful, fresh, and redemptive rendering of theology that invites an uncommon and courageous love. With a poetic blend of passionate activism, holy lessons, and Godly love, Jeff takes us on a soul journey from our unjust and inhumane death chambers to the throne of grace. This book dares to imagine God's image and personhood executed with each state sanctioned taking of life. Such daring and such love, our soul and our society desperately need in these tragic times."

— Estrus Tucker, Mystic

"Jeff continues to point us toward the justice of God with words of grace and challenge. His work with people who live on death row calls us to examine our commitments to life and love for all of God's people, especially our efforts to abolish the death penalty."

— Leah Grundset Davis, Alliance of Baptists

"In a world that still begets violence for violence, Rev. Jeff Hood witnesses to the radical notion that murdering a murderer is not the Christian way. As a sincere follower of Jesus Christ, Jeff has led many nonviolent protests against the death penalty, particularly in his home state of Texas. His witness is not one to bring attention for himself, but rather to focus redemptive attention to the dark underbelly of our human desire for revenge. I admire Jeff's commitment to love and pray for his ongoing work to abolish the death penalty."

— Bojangles Blanchard, Highland Baptist Church, Louisville

"I first met Jeff in Austin in 2014, as he finished the last leg of a 200-mile protest walk from Livingston. He was tired, yet focused and compelling. Since then I have watched him remain dedicated to abolition in a state where we need it desperately. Jeff is a passionate truth-teller, authenticating his rhetoric with love in action. I am repeatedly led into a holy discomfort by his writing. May discomfort find you as well."

— Amelia Fulbright, Labyrinth Progressive Student Ministry, Austin

"Have you ever felt like going across the line? The line is the place where your beliefs meet your calling to act. Which injustice happening in our bizarre world sickens you to the point of illness? Maybe that sick feeling has meaning, or your anger, or your righteous disgust has purpose? Rev. Dr. Hood is bold within these pages to invite you to accompany him on such a transformational walk. This is the difficult journey to decide to defeat our immoral practice of executing our criminal neighbors. Hood does not shy away from any ethical societal contradictions, unpleasant details, nor his intimate wrestlings with his own humanity nor his mental and emotional limitations. He believes, as do many blessed, impassioned radical Christians, that the answers must come from our gathered sacred humanity, that we must gather the Godly resources and when they are depleted, ask for replenishment, forgiveness and keep walking. Hood is also sober and most adult about our national childlike fantasies about the death penalty. If you are on the 'abolition' road with him, this will assist and inform your work. If you are on one of the thousand other roads to our collective freedom, this poetic journal may encourage you to see and feel what is going on just a few blocks over.

— Duncan E. Teague, Abundant Love Unitarian Universalist Ministry, Atlanta

"I believe all life is sacred, all are made in the image of the Divine, so I see all life as precious. In *The Execution of God: Encountering the Death Penalty,* Jeff takes you on a ride of experiencing the sacred nature of life. Jeff produced a mindful, spiritual journey that is easy to understand, and challenging. This book will disrupt you on levels you may not even think about. I found this book helpful in giving me a deeper voice against the taking of any human life. Be ready to be disrupted."

— John O'Keefe, author of *The Naked Jesus* and *DISRUPT: Everything Changes*

"Dr. Hood is a powerful witness to a love that refuses to allow anyone to be defined by his/her worst mistakes."

— Craig Hunter, Trinity Presbyterian Church, Denton, Texas

"The Rev. Dr. Jeff Hood, who is at once minister, social justice activist, and death penalty abolitionist, offers theological honesty, depth, and inquiry that express dissatisfaction with traditional, frequently stuffy, status quo-affirming beliefs that congratulate people of faith more than they challenge them. *The Execution of God* will cause readers to enter a zone of religious, political, and social discomfort that has the potential to help them reexamine their faith and the roles they play within structures and institutions that confer worth and dignity on some while withholding such from others. As discomfort often sets the stage for innovation, this book is an essential read."

— Jack Sullivan, Jr., First Christian Church of Findlay, Ohio

"Dr. Hood uncovers complex theology to reveal the plain truth of love: urgently and among a chorus of liberation to walk away from a culture of killing. We are asked to move beyond the conformity of hate and death to the sacredness of our shared humanity. To know that God dwells in the darkest places, and specifically with those on death row, is to see abundant life and value in lowly places. Encountering the notions 'God is on death row' and 'God is an abolitionist' is to be humbled by the Truth of our shared and specific human dignity. The possibility, hope, and deep insight Hood provides cannot have come at a better time."

— David Ragland, The Truth Telling Project of Ferguson

"Bold. Spirit moving. Again and again Jeff Hood puts his mind, heart, and body into the work of abolition. *The Execution of God* demands that we see God in those who are executed—to extend our love to both them and to the executors. Hood urges us to shift cultural norms that seek revenge and death and recognize God's grace as an opportunity to prioritize life. Walking with Jeff Hood for abolition of the death penalty in Ohio was an honor. As a community, we carry the stories, the divinity, and the humanity of each person living and executed on death row. May we all continue to walk with bold strides and challenge the status quo of society's death machine as Hood passionately calls us to join him."

— Allison Reynolds-Berry, Intercommunity Justice & Peace Center, Cincinnati

"Jeff Hood guided me to death row. Through the voices of the condemned, I am forever changed."

— Larry James, CitySquare, Dallas

"In *The Execution of God* Jeff Hood has spoken for not only the condemned headed to execution, but also for all of us. With often irreverent language and images, he asks questions of the biblical text many have thought but been reluctant to say aloud. He questions our distorted theologies constructed to support our thirst for killing, and he bids Christians to examine our calling—to love God with all that we are, and to love our neighbors as ourselves. We all have a little God in each of us, and Jeff Hood gets close enough to the condemned to affirm this *imago dei* truth about all—no exceptions. And he questions each of us: 'Are we killers?' Or are we followers of Jesus committed to forgiveness, reconciliation, and restoration walking in the loving path of life? We must choose. The restoration of our world hangs in abeyance waiting for our response."

— Paula Dempsey, Alliance of Baptists

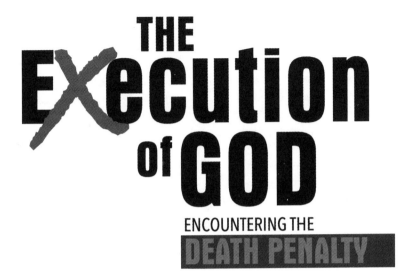

THE EXecution of GOD

ENCOUNTERING THE
DEATH PENALTY

JEFF HOOD

chalice
press

Saint Louis, Missouri

An imprint of Christian Board of Publication

Scripture quotations are directly quoted or adapted from the *New Revised Standard Version Bible,* copyright © 1989 National Council of the Churches of Christ in the United States of America. Used by permission. All rights reserved.

Covert art: Emily Hood
Cover design: Jesse Turri
Photo on back cover: Natalie Roberson

ChalicePress.com

Print ISBN: 9780827208513
EPUB: 9870827208520 EPDF: 9780827208537

Printed in the United States of America

CONTENTS

For the Executed

PREFACE

IS GOD A KILLER? I don't think so. Well, then again, I don't know. I guess I should stick to talking about things that I know. What is there to actually know? When you get right down to it, I guess we all only know a little. If we just stuck with what we know, we wouldn't be able to produce much. This wild collection of words flows out of unknowing. Revelation isn't about spaces of knowing. Revelation is about spaces of unknowing. In the chaos, we find God or God finds us. This is a book about God... The *dead* God... The *executed* God.

THEOLOGY IS A LOST ART.

Experimentation is about recovery.

The Execution of God is an experiment concerned with the recovery of art.

THEOLOGY CALLS OUT TO US. Listen wider. Can't you feel the beauty of it all? Look over there. Can these words live? They don't seem to fit. There must be something wrong. Prophesy to the words! Tell the words to be filled with life. The majesty of art began to revive the words. The ground was shaking. The earth was quaking. Dead words of theology began to rise and bring forth new life. In the midst of it all, the voice of God and the voice of abolition became one. Theology ushered in a creation free from the horrors of the death penalty.

BALLADS TELL STORIES. Listen. God is in the melodies. There is a song in this text. Every so often, a short grouping of verses arises out of the text to collectively bring forth something magical. The embedded ballad pulls at the eyes, to get to the ears, to pierce the heart. Literally and figuratively, there is a new song in this text. *Sing out! Do you feel it? Sing out! Do you know it? Sing out! Are you ready? God's abolition is at hand. No more* ex-e-cu-tions *in our land.*

THE END IS NEAR! What does the end look like? In our minds, we must make a way out of no way. We must find the end and go there. The end is about giving everything we've got. The apocalyptic amalgamations in this text are abolition amalgamations. Grab the revelations of abolition and hold on tight. God uses these types of stories to make sure that we don't get left behind.

THIS IS NOT A NORMAL BOOK. I ain't gonna study killing no more. Normal is always about killing. From our economic systems, to crime, to war, to a wild assortment of other manifestations, I can think of nothing more normal in our world than killing. I'm trying to get away from killing. I'm interested in getting back to life. Now, real life is always something other than normal. With the knowledge that normal always leads to more dead bodies, I set out to write something queer. I have no doubt that I did.

Rev. Dr. Jeff Hood
October 2016

DEATH NOTES

Behold, the heavens opened up and I saw the chamber of death. I could hardly believe my eyes. In the center of the room, I saw a gurney.

Death Is the Beginning

"In the beginning..." -Genesis 1:1

"There will be silence!" "Sit down! Sit down!" "The charge is murder!" Death is natural. Murder is not. Do you recall the execution of God? You were there. So was I. We witnessed it all. We watched God being led into court. We heard the incriminating testimony. We listened to the damning details about God's past. We cringed at the description of the crime. We wanted the demise quicker than the law would allow. The guilty verdict moved us. The sentence sent us into a pandemonium of elation. "Death!" In time, we forgot about it. Later, we rediscovered the joy of murder in the days leading up to the execution. We told everyone that death was too lenient. We watched as God was led into the chamber and strapped down. We saw the needle draw blood. We were thirsty for more. We listened to God's surprising words of forgiveness. We watched the poison flow. We waited to feel better. We didn't. We felt empty. The execution of God only made us worse. God was dead. Who would save us now?

God died
It wasn't no suicide
Look, isn't it plain to see
It could've been you or me

Move

"*...move...*" -Acts 17:28

God has countless names. Not long after "the shirt" arrived, I dropped by my grandparents' house. Emblazoned in white letters across the front of the blue fabric was the cry, "I am Troy Davis." Many decades prior, in a racially charged trial with a whole host of problematic evidence, Davis was convicted of killing Officer Mark Allen MacPhail in Savannah, Georgia. As the time of Davis' execution drew closer, I felt more and more drawn to the case. On that day, I walked in the front door. Even though my grandparents were prejudiced against a whole host of people in a variety of ways, I didn't think anything of wearing the shirt in their presence. Not long after I entered, my grandmother screamed out, "Oh, my God!" Feeling like a fit of rage was next, I froze. Though I felt like I already knew the answer, I asked, "What is it?" With tears in her eyes, my grandmother said, "Troy Davis is the name of my brother who was paralyzed in the war." Even though she knew my shirt had nothing to do with her brother, the slogan "I am Troy Davis" touched her core. When I told her what the shirt was really about, she instructed me not to tell my grandfather. I didn't. When I was about to leave, my grandmother looked me in the eyes and said, "We all have a little God in us... Perhaps we all have a little Troy Davis in us too." Could the God in a white Troy Davis and the God in a black Troy Davis be the same God who is the God in us all?

In the midst of the juxtaposition between black and white in my community, everyone I knew supported executions. In fact, I think most of the people wanted them to happen more often. This is also an accurate description of my family. We loved Jesus and, therefore, we thought we needed blood. I guess the death penalty turns us all into vampires or maybe it's Christianity that actually does that with its sermons and songs about the blood of Jesus. The execution was close. Christians were the biggest proponents for killing Troy Davis. I couldn't figure out why. Regardless, I placed a tremendous amount of trust in one Christian in particular. An attorney from our community sat on the Board of Pardons and Paroles. While all the other folks on the Board very well *could've* been the Christians they *claimed* to be, I knew for a fact that at least one member was. For many years, I'd seen his fruit with my own eyes. Through it all, I kept telling myself that I didn't have anything to worry about. I didn't trust all those other cats. I trusted this attorney. In the midst of crisis, we should expect God to show up in Christians. Our expectations are often executed. I'll never forget that night. Darkness closed in. Death was the only God.

Georgia is a mysterious place. Evil rises and falls like the morning dew. You can't really catch it. Before you know it, it's gone. If you can't catch it, it's not real to the average viewer. Public officials in Georgia have a way of calling themselves Christians and avoiding the dawn. For, if they rise too early, evil might be seen for what it is. No one woke up early that day. Public officials talked about God and rushed toward killing. Evil was all around. I'd never been to an execution before. The drive was dark and ominous. Desperate for updates, I left the radio on. Over and over, I prayed for God to move. I couldn't figure out what was happening. Fear was closer than God ever was. Somewhere in there, I heard that the Board of Pardons and Paroles denied clemency for Troy Davis. The attorney, I knew, wouldn't stop there. Christians don't stop. I pulled the car up as the sun was setting. I parked across from a gas station with a burger joint in it. Looking out the windows, the people stuffing their faces with meat didn't seem to notice the crowd gathering. I kept pushing toward the prison.

Light remained longer than I thought it would. It was as if the sun refused to move. Looking up, I felt like the very cosmos was trying to expose what was going on. I didn't get any further than Highway 36. Hundreds of law enforcement officers met me there. I'd never seen so many batons and shields. Slap after slap to their shin guards warned the gathered demonstrators that violence was there for whoever wanted it. Multiple people took them up on the offer. I just prayed. More law enforcement in riot gear showed up. I thought they were coming across the street. No one did. I figured the attorney I knew was doing all that he could. Holding a sign that read "The World is Watching," I stepped out into the street as far as I could. In the midst of the chaos, an old man driving a tan van purposefully turned into the crowd. After he struck me with his side mirror, he had the nerve to get out and say that I was trying to destroy his car. The wild scene morphed into pandemonium when word reached us that Troy Davis had been granted a brief stay from the United States Supreme Court. It felt like a resurrection. Maybe God wasn't so absent after all. Between the attorney I knew and the Supreme Court, I knew we had this. I knew God was working. I was wrong.

Joy quickly turned into mourning. We knew a murder was about to take place. Darkness descended on my heart. My psyche grew foggy. The United States Supreme Court dropped the stay and allowed the execution to proceed. We'd all failed. While murders happen all the time, tremendous numbers of people were watching this time. The various lights of the protests filled the night. I tried to convince my brain that these lights represented a divine light. My heart knew better. Divinity was gone. I put down my "The World is Watching" sign. I couldn't lie anymore. The world didn't care about the killing of Troy Davis. If the world cared at all, they would've stopped it. A woman shrieked at the top of her lungs, "They killed an innocent man!" Feeling like I'd lost control of my body, I crumpled over. I had to get back to the car. Struggling to be the pastor I was trained to be, I stopped beside a crying young woman and reminded her that God was with her. Looking up at me with tears flowing, she managed, "God was just executed... Move."

It was the night that murder won
We killed a native son
We're the ones who've killed so long
Georgia what's gone wrong

Moving

God created us in God's image... -Genesis 1:27

Theology is always the weapon of the executioner. In order to kill, one has to find a way to believe that killing is a necessity.

Christians are experts at such problematic believing. We manage to turn killers into monsters while turning ourselves into killers. We forget that they, like us, were made in the image of God. However, monsters are easier to kill than God. The problem is, *God* is always in the monsters. God don't make no monsters. God makes children created in the divine image. Every time we carry out one of these executions, we are executing God. We are executing the image of God in that person. The only way that you can execute God is if you have a theology that is contrary to what God teaches. We do. We desperately need something else. Theology is the only way back.

God created us. God created us in God's very image. Theology begins and ends with God's image. Persons are created for relationship with the entity that they reflect. Theology must uplift the divine or it is not theology. You cannot uplift the divine without uplifting the divine within. Theology is about the striving to know God through deeper knowledge of our creation in God's image. How can one human reflection of God be better or worse than another? The only way that we can carry out these executions is to believe that the image of God in a person has been so totally destroyed that the person is no longer deserving of life. Who gets to make such a decision? The answer *should be:* God and God alone. When God had the chance to kill the first persons who unleashed evil in our cosmos, God showed grace. In the fullest revelations of the divine, God heals. Why do we kill when God consistently chooses to heal? We are killing in the name of a God who daily shows restraint. We're killing God's image all around us. We're killing our ability to see God's grace through the restoration of God's image. The death penalty is about God's image. We don't believe that the image of God is present in all people. If we did, we wouldn't be killing God.

People walk around insecure and angry. People seem determined to destroy anything that they determine to be evil. Unfortunately, no one ever takes the time to realize that the evil without is actually evil within. The death penalty is a reflection of our desire to kill. We are ravenous for blood. We just don't know where to direct our energies. Will we destroy ourselves or someone else first? The sprint to kill the image of God is about our desire to be free. We want to do what we want to do. The image of God is too heavy a burden to carry. We go crazy looking for something else to fill the void. We want something to take the place of God. We never find it. When we realize that our search is fruitless, we kill in order to keep from dealing with the evil impulses that made us stray in the first place. The death penalty gives us an outlet. Killing the image of God in the other keeps us from killing the image of God in ourselves.

So in whose image is the death penalty created? If you listen to many Christians, you would think God created the death penalty in the divine image. Followers of Jesus kill all the time. How can this be? Christians are taught that Jesus is the complete embodiment of God's image. Did Jesus execute or was Jesus executed? In the Incarnation, God was executed. The life of Jesus is the antidote to our disgusting murderous theology. The life of Jesus is the antidote to the death penalty.

"...God is love" (1 John 4:8). In God is love, and in love is God. God is always going to be the love beyond love. God is always going to be the love so loving that we can barely comprehend it. God loves the world so much that God came and died. The problem is that we have twisted the love of God to fit our theologies. We have somehow reached a space where we can believe that God can love and kill at the same time. I can't think of anything more blasphemous. Loving and killing can't go together. Killing is evil. The death penalty is evil. It is always going to be evil to destroy the image of God. It is always going to be evil to destroy love. How can a God be love and promote killing? To believe in such a God is to divide the mind and sacrifice the mind for the blood we want. To believe in such a God is to divide the soul and sacrifice the soul for the blood we want. When so much dividing and sacrificing is going on, God is lost and so are we. The death penalty succeeds in killing not just the offender *without,* but the offender *within.* We must find a way back to love.

We've always been desperate for easy answers. Over and over, people asked Jesus for simplicity. Occasionally, Jesus gave it to them. In Matthew 22, Jesus told the people that the greatest commandment is to love God with all that you got and to love your neighbor as your self. If love is at the center of the message of Jesus, anything other than love is not Jesus. How could love not be the center of any religious message? Killing and love simply can't exist together. You can't love God and kill God. You can't love your neighbor and kill your neighbor. The greatest commandment is the great commandment against the death penalty. Executions are a failure to love. How could killing someone be anything other than a failure? To purposefully take a life is never a success. Love is the only construction that can save us. Love is the antidote to the death penalty.

We don't know people. We think we do. We even *know* we do. We're prepared to act. Our minds produce decisive judgments after brief encounters. Why do we function like this? Think about all the times we turn on the television and see someone who has committed a heinous crime. We assume that the person deserves everything he or she gets and more. Before long we are prepared to act as judge, jury, and executioner. The problem is that we really don't know the person. Most of us will never take the time to get to know anyone that we've suspected of committing a heinous crime. *We* are the dehumanizers. We feel that the more dehumanizing we *do* the less we will *be* dehumanized. We are dedicated dehumanizers. The problem with our functioning is that it is based on our lack of trust in our *own* persons. We dehumanize others because we have been dehumanized. We dehumanize others because we are afraid of what the unknown in them might reveal in us. Dehumanization is the antithesis of love. Dehumanization is the weapon of hate. Dehumanization is the primary tool of the executioner. The only way that people can execute someone is if they see something less than human in front of them. We've become expert dehumanizers. We've created processes and systems to unload and direct our fear and hate at the dehumanized. Of course, we're not the first.

The Pharisees couldn't dehumanize enough. They seemed to believe that destruction was the sole purpose of religion. Love was a false concept. Those who spent too much time on compassion were the enemies of God. Love was a waste of time. Mercy was unheard of. The Pharisees did whatever it took to dehumanize.

Rejecting the repeated advances of the Pharisees, a woman raced home. When she arrived, a Pharisee came through the front door and attacked her. When the other Pharisees saw all of her clothes ripped off, they declared her actions adultery and deemed them punishable by death. Dragging her through the streets, the Pharisees told everyone they caught her in the very act of adultery. What they didn't tell everyone is that they set her up. Regardless of how anyone arrived in their custody, the Pharisees had only one objective in mind...the death penalty. With all the energy they could muster, the Pharisees made sure the entire community knew the woman deserved execution. Sensing an opportunity to trip up Jesus, the Pharisees slung the woman at his feet. "This woman has violated the law and should be executed," the Pharisees screamed. The death penalty always begins with the battle in the court of public opinion.

Regularly, we discover the egregious sins of law enforcement. What makes us so sure that such evils have not led to the execution of innocent people? We assume that courts minimize such accidents. The problem is that the minimization of such accidents still means that innocent people are executed. I've heard that the execution of the innocent is the price we pay to live in a just and orderly society. Make no mistake, the Pharisees made similar remarks. When justice is balanced by death, we don't have any clue who the next victim will be. We only know that the death penalty will be what leads us forward, not love. Salvation comes from deconstructing the structures of execution and realizing that we are the executioners.

Our legal system sanitizes the actions of the Pharisees. How many times have we seen suspects or their pictures paraded in front of cameras? Heinous cases are always tried first in the media. We have to convince people that there's a monster in our midst. The Pharisees were able to drag the woman toward an execution because no one stopped to question the executioners. No one questions us, either. Like the Pharisees, we just keep on executing in God's name. We don't stop to consider the cost. We just want more blood. Where does that thirst come from?

Dirt rose. Heat lingered. Silence reigned. What was Jesus going to do? The world is wondering about our next move. We stand between the executioner and the condemned. We are in the same spot that Jesus was. The safe choice is to stand still. If we let someone else take the blows, we won't have to. Jesus was never safe. In the midst of certain death, Jesus moved toward the woman. There will always be the temptation to stay clean. We think that cleanliness is next to godliness. We think that cleanliness will keep us from death. We are wrong. You can't engage the world and not get dirty. God is always dirty. If the source of life is dirty, why do we spend so much time trying to stay clean? The death penalty is about cleansing. We think we can get rid of the dirt and make ourselves cleaner. We are wrong. The only way we can make ourselves whole is to restore the afflicted. We have to get dirty. Jesus knew life couldn't come from cleanliness and safety. Without hesitation, Jesus got down in the dirt.

People ran to the piles of stones. Carnage was on the menu and nobody wanted to miss the show. The Pharisees stood ready to fire. No one averted their eyes. Everyone wanted blood. Why have we always had such a desire for blood? We want carnage. One does not have to search far for proof of this fact. Those who encircled the woman wanted to kill someone, or at least be close to her death. The same is true of us. Those who want to kill someone or at least see a little blood always surround modern executions. There is a tremendous blood lust in the human race that seems to be timeless. Nothing about this makes us *human*. Killing always takes away *humanity*. We don't care. We want to kill.

Those who gather for executions are not the only problematic people amongst us. Think about all the people that the Pharisees dragged the woman past. Think about all the people that we drag the condemned past. Door after door shut. Window after window closed. We go deeper into the house. We go further into the business. We make noise so that we don't have to hear it. We do whatever we can to resist any temptation we might have of ever considering whether what is happening is right or not. We turn our eyes. We shift our heads. We move our bodies. We just don't want to have to believe that we are part of killing someone. We would never go to an execution and probably don't even think about them. Those who ignore the cries of the condemned are just as guilty as the executioners. Jesus couldn't ignore her. Jesus got down in the dirt. Jesus stared down their stones.

We can't stop the machinery of death without being prepared to die. Jesus was. With the death penalty about to be carried out, Jesus put his body between the condemned and the executioners. If the stones had ripped, Jesus would've died with the woman. The call to life is a call to give our lives so that others might live. In refusing to move, Jesus challenged the carnage and the Pharisees dropped their stones. While death was possible, life became probable. We cannot bring about life without the possibility of death. The call of Jesus is always to go and do likewise. We are called to place our bodies between the condemned and executioners. Where do we stand? Do we participate? Do we watch? Do we ignore? Do we work? Do we get down in the dirt? Do we give our lives? Where do we stand? These questions speak beyond a political reality to our very souls. Our engagement with the death penalty speaks to our engagement with God. Do we love God enough to stop the execution? Do we want to follow Jesus? In the face of the death penalty, Jesus shows us who God is. God is always going to be down in the dirt. God is always going to be ready to die. God is for the deconstruction of anything that promotes the destruction of humanity. How can we execute people without promoting the murder of God's image? We can't. God is an abolitionist.

People dropped their stones and walked away. What did it feel like to save a life? Obviously, there's a difference between walking away disappointed that you didn't get to kill someone and walking away feeling like you've been enlightened to do the right thing. While walking away saves the life of the condemned, it doesn't save the life of the walker. While I certainly wish more people would walk away from killing, the only walking that can save the life of the walker is when the walker turns toward the condemned. The walk toward the condemned is the walk of restoration and reconciliation. We need to be restored. God restores. Love restores. God is in those we condemn. We can't be restored until we are reconciled to the ones who we have condemned. We have to choose to walk in the loving path of life, not death. The abolition of the death penalty frees us to the task. When we put down our stones and walk toward the condemned, we are finally ready to meet God.

That woman was dehumanized
Knocked down by all of their lies

Movements

"...the powers of movement were established..." -2 Esdras 6:3

Symphonies are majestic. The haunting sounds of instruments racing around and crashing into each other always rattle my soul. If people were listening to such instrumentation for the first time, they might think they were hearing chaos. There is noise crashing from every direction. The music itself testifies of timeless movements. When we open our hearts, timeless movements move us to places beyond the ability of our comprehension to describe. God is in the chaos. The timeless movements are God.

Did God know it would all turn out like this? Would God do it all over again? Is God still creating? The questions of creation call us into deeper spaces of reflection. We want to know the Creator. We want to know our creation. The death penalty should make us ask similar questions. Did God create the condemned to turn out like this? Would God create the condemned again? Is God still creating the condemned? The questions of creation should call us to deeper connection with those whom we condemn. The Creator who created the condemned is the same Creator who created us. We can understand so much about our creation by engaging the creation of the condemned. God is in there. God is on death row. God is waiting for us.

Something is just not right. We were supposed to truly live. We were supposed to be something so much more than this. What happened? We fell. We hit bottom. We didn't live up to our promise. We stumbled. We looked for God somewhere else. The birth of children gives us hope. In the eyes of a baby we see the possibility of something greater than what is. There is no one sitting on death row that wasn't once a baby. We were all babies at one point. We all represented hope at one point. What happened? Can we get that hope back? You can't answer the questions of the future until you're prepared to engage the past. Our common origin with those who are condemned to die helps us to know that we all began in hope and only by connecting with each other can we proceed in hope. We fell. We both fell. We looked for God in the wrong place and now we're paying the price. While one might argue that those on death row fell harder, the truth is that falling is falling. The abolition of the death penalty is about recognizing our fallenness in the fallenness of the condemned. God never leaves us. God's been falling with us for a long time. The good news is that God always knows the way back up.

Jesus is the damndest person I've ever known. Dropped down in a pile of shit in Bethlehem, Jesus spent his life standing for the condemned. Over and over, Jesus proves to be the incarnation of God through selfless acts of love. Matthew writes about one moment in particular. When pondering the oppressed in Matthew 25, Jesus says that he will always be with those who are in prison. Jesus is the incarnation of God. Jesus is with and in those who are in prison. Jesus is on death row. God is on death row. I can testify that God lives on death row. I've met her there many times. I've met him there many times. I've met God there many times. Though many of them are ruthless killers, God has chosen to dwell with and in them. The death row incarnation is an amazing event of mercy and grace. God is still speaking. Most people are just not close enough to the condemned to hear it.

Jesus died. Redemption flowed out of his death. In dying, Jesus showed us how to live. We are to give our lives for others. We are to be about dying everywhere we go. We are to die to our selves in order to give life to the world. We can't give life when we are busy handing out death. We've got to start dying. If we start dying like Jesus did, we will stop killing. We will be about abolition. People on death row are always about dying. Death is a constant presence for them. Maybe they can teach us a thing of two about living? Lessons on dying are also contained in the last words of the executed. In statement after statement, I've heard powerful words of God come from the gurney. Dying and God go together. God died, and so will we. Will we die for others? The redemption we find will be our own.

Something is happening. People are dreaming of a world beyond death. Something is happening. People are working for abolition no matter how many people are executed. Something is happening. People are seeking to forgive in the most heinous of circumstances. Something is happening. People are learning to love. Something is happening. The world is changing. Restoration is upon us. We must let our highest dreams go wild. We must believe that such dreams are possible. We must work to make them true. Restoration is about taking the condemned and working to restore their lives. Restoration is about allowing the condemned to restore our lives. Dreams become reality the second we start believing that restoration is possible. We can restore our world.

We can stop seeing killing as the answer to killing. We can stop pursuing the death penalty. We can stop sentencing people to death. We can stop carrying out death sentences. We can choose life. We can stop death. The restoration starts in our restoring. We are restored when we turn away from the death penalty. We will be dead until we do. We will either love God or kill God. The death penalty offers us no other options.

As the symphony plays
The hours away
We draw closer to the gurney
To begin our journey

The Beginning is Death

"For I am convinced that..." -Romans 8:38

God is in the final moments. Time is drawing to a close. Will we sit back and allow God to be executed? Will we just close our eyes? Will we turn away? Will run in fear? Will we do something? The executioner prepares for the moment. *The Execution of God* is about choosing differently. *The Execution of God* is about being different. *The Execution of God* is about making a difference. Where is our courage? The executioner just moved toward the gurney. The clock ticks. What are you going to do? There are only seconds left. Do you hear? God is lying there begging for help.

Behold, I was drawn deeper into the chamber of death. I saw God being led to the gurney. Desperate for understanding, I pushed in closer. I heard a voice in the distance pronounce, "This is the execution of God."

ORIGINS

Behold, I was transported from the chamber. The curtain was drawn. From a distance, I could see God battling Evil.

Beginning

"In the beginning..." -Genesis 1:1

"You are a worthless piece of shit." "You will never amount to anything." "You are nothing." God heard the words repeatedly. The hand came down across the face of God. Blood rushed everywhere. The divine nose shattered. How will we explain the abuse? I can't turn my head. "What happened?" Pain played out again and again. God decided to abuse others.

"Follow all of my voices." "Cut your arm." "Stick the needle in." "Listen to me. Or me. Or me. Listen to me." "Trust no one." Darkness grew in the mind of God. The brain was unable to accept anything but darkness. Urges to destroy crept in. God started to act on those urges. God became addicted.

"I just need help!" The foot kicked God hard enough to break the divine ribs. 'I just need help!" The foot kicked God again. "I just need help!" Nobody listened. So God decided to start inflicting the same level of pain. There was nothing to harm. There was only God. There was only darkness. In the absence of light, God decayed from the inside out. Rot was the only evidence of life that God had. Destruction was the only thing that could bring God back. Unfortunately, destruction is addicting.

The idea crept up on God. Visions of mayhem went round and round. Desperate to resist, God reached for the light. There was no light. Everything was dark. Thrown about, God grabbed the divine mind. Trying to subdue it, God slung the entirety of the divine being back and forth. Screaming out, God released the plan. The mechanism was in motion. Though God considered stopping it, God knew that the slaughter of the innocent was the only way to make it stop. The beast must be fed. Despite constant hesitation, God intended to feed it.

If we are to believe the scriptures, God is the first murderer. Think about the innumerable people who have died since creation. Maybe that's why we're so comfortable with the death penalty. How can we hold anyone but God be responsible for death? Does God deserve the death penalty? Unless we are transformed by the love of God, it's hard to believe otherwise.

In the beginning, God created murder. God needed something to hunt. For days, God created obstacles for the encounter. Light, dark, water, terrain, other animals and a variety of other conditions were put in place. The Earth was truly wild. To make things interesting, Eden was created to be the safe zone. God would never kill in Eden.

After dropping two humans into Eden, God prepared for the hunt. Though God felt a moral restraint to not kill, God couldn't resist. "Don't eat of the tree or you will die!" God just put the tree there so that God would feel better about killing them. Decades passed as God hid behind a tree, waiting for the perfect moment. The desire to kill would not let go of God. Watching, God sometimes felt guilty. Blowing it off, God knew that the taste of murder would solve all of that. One day, God saw the humans go to the tree and eat. Knowing that the moment was here, God kicked the humans out of Eden. Readying his weapon for the hunt, God let the humans get a good start. Then, God hunted them until they were dead.

Unable to shake the urge to keep killing, God roams the Earth, taking people out. God has fallen victim to a depraved mind and wicked heart. God is the most prolific killer to ever exist. Perhaps due to a deranged childhood, God created the death that comes for us all. God has no soul. God is a monster. God is addicted to murder. God is not human.

"We caught God!" Interestingly enough, no one seemed to care. Everybody was just like God. After driving a short distance from the jail, God was arraigned and prepared for trial. Realizing the charges, no one wanted to represent God. The courts appointed an attorney. Throughout the trial, God's attorney slept and did nothing. The jury stayed out for just a second. "Guilty!" Just a few minutes later, the sentence was read, "Death!" Everyone present cheered. The prosecutor told the media, "An eye for an eye, and a tooth for a tooth." Families of victims wrote in to demand a swift execution of justice. God knew that killing was wrong. God also knew that God would kill again. The creation of the death penalty begins with a killer named God.

God got loose
Where's that poison juice?

Reason

"...of the knowledge of good and evil." -Genesis 2:9

Murderers are simply emulating the greatest murderer of them all. Why should we view God any differently than the murderers on death row? Our stories are important. We cannot back away from them. We must look straight into the evidences of what God has done. Our stories are evidences that demand a verdict. Spirituality begins in our Genesis.

What was going on in the mind of God before our creation? The question beckons us to a place of dreams. Were the thoughts of God light or darkness? So often we put God in a place of perfection that God has not asked to be put. We dream of our beginnings and put ourselves in that place of perfection too. The problem with beginning in perfection is that truth is never perfect. We have never known truth to be perfect. The existential nature of all that is or will ever be is never perfect. We know this from our own experiences. We are made in the image of God. We exist in a mixed state of light and darkness. Why would the origin of the image be any different?

Questions of origin are fundamental to any conversation on the death penalty. What question does God ask when God is condemned? What question does the condemned ask when the condemned is condemned? There is only one question that comes to mind. There is only one question that unites us all: *Who do you say that I am? Who do you say that God is? Who do you say that we are?* Questions of origin guide the way.

"Crimes against humanity!" God is condemned to die. God is strapped to the gurney. The hour is upon us. The poison is ready. God looks over. "Do you have any final words?" God leans toward the glass. "Who do you say that I am?" The question lingers. Mechanisms are in motion. God dies. The deed is done. The only problem is that everyone is wondering who they just killed: "Did we get the right person?" The question continues to give them pause. The question continues to give *us* pause.

Do we know the right God? Do we know the God that we think we know? *God is perfect. God is omnipotent. God is holy.* Statements like these don't make sense in the light of the image of God. If you want to know what God is like, look at the condemned. The murderers tell us more about God than any theological text. "Who do you say that I am?"

There is a body on the gurney. What difference does it make whose it is? There is a body on the gurney. What difference does it make who put it there? There is a body on the gurney. Does it matter what type of body? There is a body on the gurney. Someone is about to die. We spend too much time analyzing what's happening and not enough time saving the body on the gurney. In the midst of our staring, the body starts to turn. "Who do you say that I am?" If this body has any connection to God, then it is valuable beyond all imagination. If this body doesn't have any connection to God, then is has no value. Is there a body not created in the image of God? The question comes again: "Who do you say that I am?" Our new creation is always found in finding God. Sometimes it takes a few questions to get there. Creation begins in the condemned. Creation begins in the past. Do you hear our searchings?

God breathed life
God breathed death
Now, we're stuck
Shit, what's left?

Church

"Who told you that you were naked?" -Genesis 3:11

"Where's my underwear?" "Where's the soap?" "How long do we have to stay?" Sunday mornings were always a mess. We repeatedly ran into each other before actually getting into the car. Then, there were things we remembered once the car was in motion. If we were just around the block, we would return for a Bible. No matter where we were, we returned for any essential article of clothing. Now that I think about it, the Bible and essential clothes were the only things we ever turned around for. Truth be known, I don't ever remember leaving for church without forgetting something. The creation of our ecclesial experiences doesn't seem all that different from God's creation. God keeps turning around until creation is right. God might have made some mistakes, but God ain't going to leave us high and dry.

"What's that smell?" After some investigation, we found two rats in the sticky trap. We decided to throw the entire trap away. Right after we picked up the trap, one of the rats started moving. We were terrified. Unable to touch the trap again, we waited for our teacher to arrive. Mr. Clay was a loud, burley man known for teaching boys how to grow into men. Being the introvert that I was, I wanted to have nothing to do with him. Knowing that Mr. Clay would force me go down the tallest slides and swing on the most ridiculous ropes, I literally wanted nothing to do with him. Despite my protests, my parents made my church class a requirement. By the time that Mr. Clay arrived, ten boys had gathered around the sticky trap. We were all daring each other to get closer and closer. One of the young men slipped and actually got the sticky trap stuck on his shoe for a minute. Everyone squealed in delight. I started to realize that I was troubled. I didn't like watching the rat suffer. I also didn't want to be a wimp. Before I could figure out how to handle the situation, Mr. Clay arrived. After ascertaining what was going on, Mr. Clay stomped over and smashed the rat with his heavy black boot. I believe I actually saw the rat's eyeball pop out. When Mr. Clay saw that I was horrified, he loudly responded, "What's the problem, Hood? Don't believe in the death penalty?" I didn't even know what he was talking about.

"God invented the death penalty." Being the fundamentalist of fundamentalists that he was, Mr. Clay had to make sure all of us boys believed in the death penalty. In the midst of his rant, I finally figured out what the death penalty was. Pointing at an old painting of fire and destruction, Mr. Clay started talking about Sodom and Gomorrah. "Do you remember the story of Sodom and Gomorrah?" Most of us didn't. Then, Mr. Clay started talking about how God executed the community for being too effeminate: "Believing in the death penalty is part of being a man. We get to choose who lives and dies." Even at the height of Mr. Clay's soaring rhetoric, I wasn't convinced. "Wouldn't it have been more ethical to try to save the rat's life?" "Hood...silly questions like that tell me that you have a long way to go before you're walking with God." I didn't believe him. I thought he was crazy. I still do. God seems to be so much closer to those trying to save life rather than those trying to kill.

The rat got stomped
And I got saved
We listened to a dumbass
For the rest of the day

Matter

"...God [was] walking in the Garden..." -Genesis 3:8

Eden was so full of life. Why did God let us leave? The quick answer has always been that we *chose* to leave. I've never believed that. I believe God left *with* us, on purpose. God knew that we would never last in the perfection of Eden. God wanted to be with us no matter what the cost. Humans were made in God's very image. How could God leave God's self? God couldn't kill humans, because God couldn't kill God's self. God was in the humans because the humans were in God. The humans could never leave because God was always in them. The image of God is a total covenant. God doesn't believe in the death penalty because God doesn't believe in destroying God. The image of God is the core of any opposition to the death penalty. Does our matter *matter*? How could our matter not matter? Our matter is divine. We are made in the very image of God. You cannot follow God without believing that God is in the matter of humans all around you. God is in the condemned because matter is divine.

God doesn't want humanity to be alone. God chases us. God joins us. God doesn't want the condemned to be alone. God chases them. God joins them. God is not our enemy. God is not our judge. God is in us. God ran out of the gates of Eden and has been with us ever since. How could God destroy God's self?

"God led the annihilation of the Canaanites." I don't believe that shit. For a long time, I was terrified by the idea that God's commanding of the slaughter of the Canaanites might have actually happened. If it was true, I know that I'd never be able to reconcile a loving God with a slaughtering God. "God got angry and asked them to kill everyone." From an early age, I encountered this vicious story. The first time I heard it, my teacher blamed it on the "anger of God." While I'd seen anger before, I couldn't imagine anything that would make me angry enough to slaughter a bunch of people. Raising my hand, I said, "Didn't God love the Canaanites?" The teacher replied, "God loves us enough to kill us." Even then, I knew this logic was shaky. "Why didn't God just change their hearts?" "Killing is sometimes the only option." I grew up in a world of assumed orthodoxy that thought that killing was often the only option. Such shitty theology informs our modern death penalty.

If one is able to believe that God did do all that killing in scripture, then they believe in a divided God. Humans carry the image of God. If God is killing humans, then God is killing God's self. How could God possibly kill God's self? The stories of God killing defy what we know about our creation. Matter *matters*. God didn't create us to kill us. God created us to be God's image in us. If God can't kill God's self, how can we kill each other? We can only kill each other by denying the God in the other in order to kill that person. Such killing has nothing to do with God. Such killing is evil. God can't command the killing of God. How could God ever be for the death penalty? We are talking about a God that is with us. Why would God want to kill God's self? Our very creation cries out against the death penalty.

God told everyone
Be still
It's time to kill

Joy

"...become like one of us..." *-Genesis 3:22*

In my earliest years, I learned about executions. Occasionally, I'd watch television with my parents. One time, I caught the aftermath of an execution. I heard a man saying: "I've never felt such joy. I wish they could kill him twice." After asking my parents what an execution was, I sat there in astonishment. How could anyone be joyful about someone being killed? I was disturbed. "Forgiveness isn't for me. I find joy in justice." I remember hearing that line from a leader at our church. We were talking about whether it was ever right to kill someone. Christian orthodoxy has often treated forgiveness as if it has an expiration date or can be maxed out. Justice is about loving your neighbor as you love your self. How can forgiveness ever run out? Does the forgiveness of God ever run out? There is no justice in an execution. How can you love your neighbor and execute them? "God is the source of all joy." Our preacher talked to us about where joy comes from. I had a good idea about what I believed about the source of joy. One time, I heard a soldier talk about how he got no joy out of killing people. Then, I heard that joy and killing don't mix. God ain't involved in killing people. Joy ain't either.

God is incarnate in those we kill. When the crime is committed, God is there. When the trial takes place, God is there. When the isolation occurs, God is there. There is no other way to say it. God is there. Joy is found in knowing God. We cannot know joy without knowing God. Our hearts expand at the feeling of joy. Our minds explode at the knowledge of joy. Our bodies are energized when we meet joy. The experience is overwhelming. God and joy are so inextricably linked that you cannot find one without the other. There is joy in this world. There are places were God's presence is so real that one cannot miss the possibility of joy in such a place. Joy is found in the marginalized and oppressed. Joy is found in those who are left out. Joy is found in the condemned. Joy is found in the souls who inhabit death rows. In those souls, God is in prison. In those souls, God is implicated in the crime. In those prisons, God is real. Joy is found in the realness of God.

Joy is a funny word to use for the lives of those on death row. Most would describe their plight as "hell." Maybe I'm not even talking about those who inhabit death row. I don't want to erase their struggles or hardships. I'm talking about the potential for tremendous pleasure when one encounters God. Maybe the creation of joy comes from the God in the condemned meeting the God in you. Joy is found in connecting God to God. Joy is found in following the will of God. Surely, one cannot love God and stay away from the condemned. God is in prison and we will either visit God there or we will die. Joy is about being made into something not getting something. Let's grab hold of such revelations and find joy. I think I see it. Joy is created when we have the audacity to believe that God is in those we call monsters. Joy is created when we realize that we don't have to kill anymore. We are creators with God. We are creating a newer world. We are partnering with other killers to create joy.

Every so often
Joy gets lost

Transference

"...in our image..." -Genesis 1:26

Letting go of our humanity is what frees us to be. We spend our whole lives trying to be what we are told to be. This is a failed endeavor. No one is going to call you to be more than you are. No one except God. We have to transcend the limitations of our category. We have to learn to be free in the midst of prisons. Transference happens when divinity meets divinity and greater divinity becomes activated. In the flow of God, we find the courage to think differently. We ask questions with answers beyond belief. Have we always existed?

Existence is an important question. What are we made of? Does someone become less of a person when they commit a crime? Does someone become less of a person if they fall victim to a crime? What is eternal? What will never end? In those questions is found our composition: we were created from God. Is it right to say that we were created? If we are from God, then certainly we are from eternity. That which embodies us has always existed. The hand of God creates us. We are created in the image of God. There is eternality about us. We have always existed. There is divinity within. The greater activation of our divinity comes when we meet divinity in the other. This is the moment of transference.

Not all sacred moments are moments that we want to exist. Amidst all of the evil that is committed by persons on death row, I'm convinced that divinity met divinity in the midst of their crimes. People interlocked in a moment of tremendous evil are not defined by that evil. God is bigger than even the most heinous things that we do. The transference of divinity always happens when divinity meets divinity. How could it not? There is always a flowingness of divinity occurring between us. God is in us. We cannot kill God. We cannot destroy the God in each other. We are created in the image of God. Evil will not win. God is being transferred even when love is not. Transference is about salvation. God takes our evil and transforms it into divinity. To deny God's presence in the midst of evil is to deny our creation in God's image. God is and will always be the great presence in times of trouble. God is the victim. God is the killer. God is in and with us all. Our creation brings about our transference. Our transference helps us to understand the interconnectedness of us all.

While transference is about divinity meeting divinity, it is also about transcending situations of evil. When a killer strikes, God does too. Divinity meets divinity and seeks to rescue both the evil and the innocent. In our creation, God placed a hunger for God within us. Should we not hunger to know the God in the evil *and* the innocent? Does God not love all of humanity? Do we believe that God loves us? If God doesn't love the condemned, how could God love us? God loves the world. God's love for us is intimately tied to God's love for the killers on death row. If all are evil, God can't love anyone any more or less. Since God's love is flowing in and out of all people, God's love for us is transferred through the very people we are trying to kill. Can you feel the love coming through the serial killer? Who are the real serial killers amongst us?

Transference is a really strange bird
That silly idea went and taught me the word

Evil

"...the serpent was more crafty than any other..." -Genesis 3:1

We kill people all the time. We kill by our inactions. We don't feed the hungry. We don't provide drink to the thirsty. We don't visit our prisons. We don't provide shelter for the stranger. We don't provide healthcare. We don't provide educations. We have so much and share so little. We are evil. The evil does not end there. We kill by our actions. We accumulate guns so that we will get the opportunity to repay evil for evil, or maybe even murder for murder. We are just waiting until it is our turn to shed blood. Through guns, missiles, drones, and a whole host of other weaponry, we kill people all over the world. Murder is so routine in our society that we don't even think about it. By the time one gets to the death penalty, we have killed so many people by so many other means that it doesn't seem like that big of a deal to kill again. So many people have been executed that people don't even notice anymore. If you turn on the television or radio following an execution, there might not even be a news report about what has transpired. Every citizen has murdered someone, and nobody even realizes that they're culpable. No one realizes that they've committed a tremendous act of evil. Nobody cares.

The greatest evil that anyone can commit against another person is to take away that person's humanity. Killers regularly try to commit such evil. The first thing that happens after a heinous crime is that everyone starts using words like monster or crazy. These words strike fear into the general populace and dehumanize the condemned. The accused becomes the condemned before any trial or criminal proceedings ever happen. By the time the accused gets into the courtroom, the game has already been fixed. Often, the next steps are just a formality. By the time the jury gets the case, prosecutors have used some of the same lines they've used in public. By the time the sentence of death is handed down, the condemned has been dehumanized enough that death seems like a worthy option. By the time of the execution, the condemned has been dehumanized to the point that nobody even cares that a killing is about to take place. Killers have to dehumanize their victims in order to kill. The greatest evil that anyone can commit against another person is to take away that person's humanity.

Evil cannot triumph. God cannot be torn from the human experience. God is with us. God cannot be taken out of us. God is within all killers.

We don't commit a greater evil on a regular basis that rivals the death penalty. It's not that we don't kill or destroy lives in higher volume in other ways. We do. The difference between our many other offenses and the death penalty is that the death penalty is an evil that allows for a whole host of other evils. If government has the right to execute its citizens, then there is no right that it does not have. The death penalty gives room for the government to go after anyone else that it thinks is a monster. I am convinced that our unlimited use of drone warfare is directly related to our use of the death penalty. It's easy for the government to feel good about killing someone halfway across the world when they've had so much practice here. The death penalty is evil not only because killing is evil. The death penalty is evil because it helps create more evils. Life sentences seem like no big deal for judges when others are getting executed. The tale is too long to tell. The death penalty is connected to and makes room for every form of marginalization or oppression in our society. Corporate killing is the "meta" of "meta-evils." When you look at how the death penalty violates human rights, there is absolutely no other word to describe our killing creation except for one word...*evil*.

God got lost
Just trying to heal
The evil down here
Just wants to kill

Awakening

"...the eyes of both were opened..." -Genesis 3:7

Breathing heavy, they made it outside. Would God be there to meet them? Would they be alone? Something seemed to be chasing them. Alone, they felt like they could see everything. Much was frightening. Much was beautiful. Everything simply was. The magic surprised them. When they ate of the tree, they thought it was over. Now, they felt like they were just beginning. Beauty was everywhere. Evil came around occasionally. Regardless, they knew how to fight back. They were woke.

The awakening is about encountering evil and recognizing it for what it is. When we wake up, we have to leave. We cannot stay around those who pretend that there is nothing wrong with the world. There are countless people executed all over the world on a daily basis. We can't stay in the shelter of paradise when we encounter evil. There are too many people who need help. The condemned have committed a great evil. Just like us. The condemned were asleep. Just like us. They are trying to get woke. Just like us. The killer in them is the killer in us. We have to leave our comfort in order to find our awakening.

Holding the big bulky black box, I dreamed of all the plots, scenes, colors, and images that were coming my way. I saw my new VCR as a ticket to a different place. While everyone was rushing to buy all the new DVDs, I was very comfortable kicking it retro. I also knew how much cheaper tapes were. High school was pretty rough. While everyone else was experimenting with drinking and sex, I was trying to find Jesus. It was a pretty boring experience most of the time. During lunch one day, I interrupted a conversation about DVDs to say, "I chose VCR. Like vinyl, the quality is so much better using the older device."

Driving home from school, I decided to stop at the movie store. For over an hour, I looked through the discount tapes. I promised myself that I wouldn't spend more than two dollars on any one tape. I also committed that I wouldn't buy a tape that I wasn't going to watch more than twice. I found many tapes that I felt ethical about. After more than an hour, I decided it was time to go. Just as I was about to leave, a title grabbed my eyeballs: *Dead Man Walking*. Honestly, I thought the movie was a portrayal of the final days in the life of Christ. I guess it could be. Regardless, I flipped the box over to see what the film was about. Within seconds, I was transported to death row. Even though I was very much for the death penalty, I thought the movie might be worth taking a chance on. Flipping the box back over, I saw that it was only a dollar. I was sold. I raced home. After I ripped off the cellophane, my heart started to slowly change.

> *That dead man's walking*
> *And that dead man's talking*
> *Oh our "theys" and "mes" are getting all con-fused*
> *Are you a killer / Now's the time to choose*

Throughout my upbringing, I heard about the death penalty. My family lived in a state that had the death penalty. We went to a church that was for the death penalty. We didn't really know anybody opposed to the death penalty. Though it might sound strange, I thought that following Jesus included being for the death penalty. Every so often, an upcoming execution would get attention and everybody would start talking about the case until the person was executed. Occasionally slipping in and out conversation, the death penalty was a way of life.

On one occasion, I was over at my friend's house. In the midst of it all, my friend asked, "Do you think Jesus ever killed anyone?" I'd never thought about it before and replied, "How am I supposed to know?" Obviously listening in, my friend's dad walked up and declared, "Not only do I think that Jesus killed people, I think Jesus uses the death penalty to kill people right now." Unsure of how to respond, I didn't say much. On another occasion, I remember a youth group leader praying for the condemned to die as painfully as his victim. In conversation after conversation, it became clear to me that God had never met an execution that God didn't like. The death penalty and the faith I was raised in were inextricable. You couldn't have pulled them a part if you'd wanted to. I figured only God could do the separating. I was right. In the midst of remembering all that I'd been taught, I put the movie in. When the colors started to fill my room, I was beyond engaged. I was having a spiritual experience.

Sister Prejean reminded me of Jesus in every scene of the movie. Prejean agreed to a spiritual relationship with Louisiana death row inmate Matthew Poncelet. What was she thinking? After bonding with Poncelet, Prejean reached out to the parents of his victims. I thought that anyone on death row was a total monster. I had no idea you could even have a relationship with someone accused of such crimes. In the meantime, Prejean helped Poncelet secure a proper attorney and together they secured delays. With every delay came more life. However, despite Prejean's best efforts to prevent it, Poncelet's execution ultimately proceeded. I thought about all of the people who've tried to save lives that were about to be executed. In the film, not long before Poncelet is executed, Prejean tells him to look at her during the execution and that she will be the face of love for him. How could anyone not be touched by incarnational love such as this? During the execution, Poncelet apologizes for his crimes and tells Prejean that he loves her. I couldn't help but think that the gurney was in the shape of a cross. At the funeral, the father of one of the victims comes to pay his respects. I wondered if God had touched him? Like Jesus, Prejean tries to love everyone and lead everyone to love. In my adolescent mind, I knew I'd never seen anything like this before. I wanted to love like Sister Helen Prejean loves. Closing my eyes, I knew that anything was possible in the midst of such love. Prayer shook my heart and rattled my brain. I was amazed by it all. In the midst of those scenes, a new creation started growing within me.

A few weeks after the movie, I pulled up a chair at church school. The topic was Cain and Abel. The teacher said that humanity created murder by leaving Eden. I wasn't sure about his conclusions. I started to wonder if God might have had something to do with it. Regardless, our teacher got more and more excited the closer he got to the murder. It was almost as if he was thirsting for blood. When Cain killed Abel, my teacher wanted was hungry for revenge. I was a little frightened. My teacher expressed his frustration with the story by saying, "God wimped out and let a killer go free." Intrigued, I leaned in. I'd never considered God wimping out about anything. Someone asked, "Doesn't this call into question our views about the death penalty?" Then, one of the other folks in the class offered, "Maybe God just wanted to torture Cain." Quickly, everyone accepted the torture narrative. The teacher even declared, "The torture interpretation fits with the God that I know." I couldn't believe that everyone in the class was more comfortable with a God who commits torture than a God who shows grace in lieu of a death penalty. I knew no one in the class had seen the movie.

Salvation

"...[they might]...live forever..." -Genesis 3:22

Have you ever been saved? I have. I think my count is up to at least a million by now. Regardless, there was one place were salvation seemed to always find me: "The Tribulation Trail." The haunted trail was a dramatic interpretation of the book of Revelation. All the Christians get taken up to heaven, while all the heathens are left down on earth. Hell breaks loose. On the haunted trail, you are exposed to everything the Bible says is going to happen. The scenes of blood and gore are enough to scare the shit out of anyone. After they traumatized enough kids, I think the church finally realized it was a bad idea to begin with. Regardless, there was one scene in particular that dealt with the death penalty. In the days approaching Armageddon, people are getting executed for not taking the Mark of the Beast. There is a guillotine right up front. We are told that this is a trial of sorts. A woman is brought out screaming and yelling. Everyone cheers. When she is thrown down next to the guillotine, the commander asks her, "Are you ready to take the Mark of the Beast?" In a feeble voice, the woman replies, "I won't." Before too much more time passes, the commander screams and throws her on the guillotine. When the blade comes down, blood goes everywhere. It was enough to make you think you were watching the real thing. When the night was over, I left thinking about the evil of killing people. The death penalty felt every bit as foolish as "The Tribulation Trail." I needed to get saved and start over. I wasn't interested in any more killing. I wondered, "Has God gotten saved from all this shit yet?"

The torture of creation
The awakening of the mind
Perfect sensation
Touchin' all we left behind

A New Creation

"...God planted a garden in Eden..." -Genesis 2:8

Matching the description, God was quickly picked up. Two people were dead. God had a gun. Who else could have done it? In a small cell, God sat and waited. Weeks passed. God's attorney was God's only visitor. The prosecution sought the death penalty. At the end of the trial, God was placed on death row. Years passed. God was alone. When the time came, God was taken to the chamber. Strapped to the gurney, God prepared to die. Moments passed. The phone rang. God received a stay. Hearings were held. Surveillance tapes were found. Eventually, God was exonerated. Creation was back.

The people gathered to go back. Closing their eyes, each one saw a familiar face. God always joined them for trips back. Through time and space, the people traveled. In the distance, everyone saw perfection. God yelled out, "This place is not as far away as you think." Flying through it all, the people felt more at home than they ever had. Many emotions were expressed. Perfection seemed so unattainable. When it became time to leave, everyone exited. Pulling them back, God said, "Wait a second! You're not leaving. This is where you are from. This place will always be in you. You will find us when you close your eyes and seek your home." The people woke up forever changed. Each of them was a new creation.

In the midst of it all, I began to thaw. I now believed in something more than killing. I started to put the death penalty down. I started to believe that God was bigger than our desire for safety. I realized that God was leading me to my origin. I remembered. I was a new creation. God was there. The death penalty wasn't.

Behold, the curtains opened up. The battle was over. God was strapped to the gurney. Evil was ready to proceed. The countdown commenced.

CERTAINTY

Behold, I heard the crimes of God read aloud. I closed my ears. I closed my eyes. I couldn't bare it.

Sinning

"Now the serpent was more crafty..." -Genesis 3:1

"The road to hell is paved with good intentions." I agree. Which is why I try to stay away from church as much as I can. I don't believe anyone has ever been executed by anything other than good intentions. I'm convinced that the people carrying out these executions think they're doing good work. The sickness of the minds of those who execute people is never more apparent than when they get home. Can you imagine your dad killing people for a living? What if your child was there to make sure that the executed was really dead? How about your mom sticking the needle in the arm of the executed? Relationships always seem to make these conversations a little different. If you have a relationship with someone, you try with all that you are to believe that you or someone you love has the best of intentions. The problem is that we know there isn't much difference between good intentions and great evil. Executions are evil no matter what the intentions of those who participate in them are. How can killing not be the road to hell?

I've known many *killers*. The ones I would describe with such blatant language are the ones who are proud of their kills. While this is a minority of persons on death row, it is important to acknowledge that blatantly unrepentant *killers* are there too. I've met people who've committed unspeakable crimes. I've met people who've told me that they want to kill again. I've met many people who don't even understand what they've done. Many of the *killers* act with a total disregard for human life. I'll never forget one meeting in particular.

A few months ago, I was sitting on a bench at a park. The grass couldn't have been greener. The skies were the perfect canvas for the gentle breeze. My three oldest children were playing. One child was on the slide, another child was on the swing, and the last child was on the bridge. Of course, they didn't stay anywhere long. I was intently watching the steps of all of my children when I noticed that someone sat down next to me. As soon as our eyes met, he extended his hand, "Hello, I'm Max!" Dressed in running shorts and a t-shirt, Max looked like any other dad at the park. Looking up, I realized that Max had two daughters about the same age as my sons. It made me happy to see the kids playing together. No matter how much I wanted to sit there and enjoy watching my kids, I knew one of those awkward conversations was creeping around. After we sat there long enough for me to think we were just going to be able to sit there, Max said, "So, what do you do?" "I'm a pastor, writer, and activist." Before we even got well into the conversation, Max questioned, "What issue do you focus on?" "I spend a tremendous amount of energy advocating for the abolition of the death penalty. I even work with a couple of guys on death row as a spiritual advisor." Max rose up, "I count myself amongst the chief proponents of the death penalty in Texas. I've celebrated the executions of hundreds. I even celebrated the ones who were 'innocent.' No one's innocent. I wish we would execute them quicker. Killing is part of justice." With a very calm demeanor, I replied, "You sound like some of the guys I know on death row. They like killing just as much as you do."

Does God sin? The question haunts us all. How do we explain all that happens? We've always assumed that God is free of sin. We cling to some sort of hope that in perfection we will find God. What if perfection doesn't exist? If so, God would be more like us. We truly would be made in God's image. Maybe God is trying, just like us, and is just having much better luck. Throughout the old stories, we find God finding the consequences of the road paved with good intentions. Does God believe in the death penalty? The old stories certainly make it seem that God does. Or maybe we got it all wrong? Maybe somebody lost the right manuscript? Maybe the stories were written down wrong? Maybe, in "maybe" is the best place to learn about God. Maybe somewhere between metal and skin there is a clearer reality.

Is sin the pathway to the answer, or is sin the very definition of confusion? If sin is the answer, then sin is the route to God. We must sin until we discover God or until we find the answer. Shall sin abound so that God will abound? The old stories seem to speak often of sin leading to God. If sin leads to God, it seems to me that death row would be a good place to find some answers. The problem with such logic is that it assumes that there is more sin *there* than there is *here*. I wouldn't say there is more sin, but I would say that there is certainly less grace. Regardless, sin does seem to have some connection with finding answers, or even God. Is it possible to find God without sin? I think sin is just as much a part of the spiritual life as worship. The only difference is that we are trying to grow out of sin. Sin is an integral part of the spiritual life. Many folks on death row have encountered God through sin. I think we have much to learn from these sages. Many of these folks are the best spiritual guides out there. Sound confusing? In the midst of such confusion, the question of sin and confusion arises. Sin distracts us and leads us down wrong paths. Sin caused us to destroy the perfection that we had in the beginning. Sin is confusing. Perhaps, though, God is found in confusion. Throughout the old stories, we met person after person who has sinned greatly and ultimately found God in the confusion of it all. In the midst of the confusion of great sin, many of the folks that I know find something on death row that sets them free. I guess it doesn't matter if we call it God or not. I guess it just matters *that* we call it. Answers and confusions fill the old stories, just like they fill the death rows and execution chambers of our answers and confusions. Maybe in the paths of the old stories we will let the truths found in the confusions lead us to God before we kill again.

Maybe we got lost
Counting the cost
Put those answers down
Let confusion abound

Babel

"...[God] confused the language of all the earth..." -Genesis 11:9

We left together. At least, I think we did. Somewhere along the way we lost each other. Were we ever really together? Who knows? I do know that there was a moment where we started speaking differently. There had to be a time when we didn't kill each other. There had to be a time when we tried to save each other. What is it like when a killer is born? Does everyone in the delivery room scream in horror? I don't think so. People see the future in infants. We aren't killers when we're born. We're human. The language gets confusing after that.

Babel was the land of dreams. After God killed most of humanity in the Great Flood, there was a remnant left demanding answers: *Why did God kill so many? Why did God kill? Why did God save us?* The endless questions were what drove them. Exploding like a sea of stars, questions kept coming. Every new answer seemed to deliver more unknown. The people searched for God there. God always seemed to pull further and further away. Death got closer and closer. Who was doing the killing? Everyone seemed so lost. The search was the only thing that united them. A cry for unity led them to building. What were they building? While a path to God is the easy answer, the harder answer is that they were building their own answers. Everyone has expectations of what the answers should be and are willing to do whatever it takes to make it happen. The Tower got them all selfish in the same direction. Or, maybe their selfishness was simply their humanity on full display? Do you remember a day in your life were you weren't selfish? Maybe we're all just following our Creator? I guess some are better at it than others.

"The death penalty is our execution of God's execution." Though I wasn't an abolitionist, the thought of execution being so tightly interwoven in the narrative of God made me uncomfortable. The pastor expected us to simply nod our heads and agree. I couldn't. I had one question that wouldn't pass, "What about Karla Faye Tucker?" I knew that the pastor had joined with many other pastors to advocate for Tucker's clemency based on her experience of an evangelical conversation. "Tucker saw the light." I couldn't let it go at that. "I feel like you have a double standard." Confusion in the room was growing. "What's double about following the will of God?" I paused for a second. "If you believe that our executions are God's executions, you should have stayed the course and advocated for Tucker to be killed. The fact that you didn't tells me that you don't really believe what you say." Anger rose. "Don't tell me what I do and don't believe!" Looking him straight in the eyes, I replied, "I didn't have to tell you anything. You told us yourself." The leader of our group quickly ended things. The pastor expected us to agree with him on everything. We did when we started. His inability or unwillingness to answer the questions birthed the rebellion of confusion.

Everyone spoke one language. I guess they did until they didn't. Questions created the confusion. Answers were overturned. We all spoke the same language. Everyone was supposed to believe in the death penalty. Everyone was supposed to believe in God the same way. We met so that we could build *our* tower to touch God. We wanted the ultimate answer. We wanted knowledge that would make us something. We lived in a land full of answers. Questions killed the answers. Maybe there were a few people who still thought they had answers, but there was no one to share them with. The confusion of it all made the death penalty seem like it was the least of our concerns. We couldn't even get our own stories straight. We couldn't even get our beliefs straight. We ran to build our tower and everything crumbled. Thus is the result when we take life and death into our hands. If our confidence can be shaken by just one question, doesn't it seem a little reckless to kill people in the midst of our confusion? Killing isn't the answer, then—*confusion* is.

Traveling eastward, the people celebrated their unity. With each step, everyone celebrated their shared adventure. No one realized that they were speaking about their answers so much that they forgot the questions. What good are answers when you have forgotten what the original questions were? This group was full of answers. There were no questions. Answers were the only place of comfort. No one could have imagined that comfort would destroy lives. Upon arrival, the people started dreaming of a city whose tower would touch God. Immediately, people started creating bricks. There are many tools and resources that go into pursuing our answers. The bricks were made out of old stuff. The mortar was made out of old stuff. Everything was old. Everything was connected to where the group came from. Didn't anyone remember that there are answers in the past? The needles are made out of old stuff. The chemicals are made out of old stuff. Everything was connected to the beginning. Didn't anyone remember that there are answers in the past? The people weren't far removed from Eden. Instead of looking back for clues, the people built for answers. We do the same thing. We don't remember our creation in the image of God. We don't remember that we come from God. We build without any idea what we're building. Thinking that our future lies in executing each other, we develop the tools to kill so that we can kill each other. Brick after brick fell into place. The mortar worked exceptionally well. Before long, the Tower was built.

Unified language helped the people build quickly. Everybody could understand each other. Everybody could speak to each other. The problem with unified language is that it comes at a great cost. The individuality of the soul is sacrificed in the process. Everyone is expected to conform. Words become the same. We too build *our* towers of death based on unified language. Everybody can understand each other when they talk about their hate for "monsters." They all know they will be heard when they talk about killers being less than human. *Death* becomes a word that everyone can agree on. Unified language kills people quicker. Isn't that what we want?

The people I knew growing up were unified in their love for the death penalty. Though my questions had grown, I knew that I would be out of step with everyone around me. Nobody likes someone who asks too many questions. That's how we end up alone. My questions had already lost me multiple friends. I didn't live in a world where dissent was encouraged. Even though I was a college student, I was still very much under the religion of my youth. While I might have asked a question here or there, I largely toed the line. Though a little more progressive than my fellow students, I knew that unified language was important. Didn't God want us to be unified? Wasn't unity the only way to get to heaven? Didn't I have to believe like everybody else believed? I had to build like everybody else. God gave us a religion, and our job was to follow it. We built Babel. Answers were our God. The answers worked for me until they didn't. Things crashed.

Strange truths whisper to our souls. While we might be building on something else, our souls never close. Sometimes, God yanks our souls and calls us back from the abyss of the answers. I don't know how I arrived at the video, I just did. For weeks, people talked about the execution of Saddam Hussein. Of course, everyone celebrated. We'd all taken our bricks and mortar and built up to this moment for a long time. There were cries of "U-S-A!" I didn't understand why so many Christians were this excited about someone's death. I thought following God was about celebrating *life*. I could go on and on about Hussein's crimes. I could go on and on about *our* crimes. However, executions are always about one crime. The crime we commit by killing someone. I was just waking up. My heart doesn't do well with people being killed. I didn't want to go there. For many weeks, I resisted. Then, after someone told me how much joy they felt after watching the video, I decided to watch. Would I feel any level of celebration? Sitting down, I tried to prepare myself to just watch the video and be done with it. After clicking "play," I knew I would never be the same: *Thinking that they had the answer, masked men march Hussein up to the gallows and prepare to kill him. The noose is placed around his neck. With his long coat, Hussein looks more like a grandfather than anything else. The executioners attach the rope. The bottom falls out, and Hussein's lifeless body hangs by a rope.* Leaning into the computer, I was in tears. Every answer I had told me to celebrate. The answers only brought me confusion. After a few more tears hit my keyboard, I experienced a salvific revelation... *I loved him.* Though rabidly fundamentalist in many ways, and a keeper of many answers, God used the execution of Saddam Hussein to confuse my world with love.

The more we build with our answers, the higher we go with our misdirection. When we turn from our answers and live into our being, we discover our creation. We have answers within us that look more like confusion, and, in the indefensibility of it all, we find that we are perfect in our confusion. The people ran after the Tower of Babel as their answer. The problem is that they were carrying within their very souls the confusion that *is* the answer. There was no need to run after all of these created answers. The unified language came from the unified shit that they were telling each other. God is bigger than our bullshit. There was only a need to be the confusion that they were created by God to be. God knew what was going on. Sweeping down, God confused the language. The destruction of the unified language confused the situation. The people grew more holy in their individuality. They were no longer united in their bullshit. God was found in the confusion, not in the answers. As the people were scattered all over the earth, there was new opportunity to be the answer that God created them to be. The people had the opportunity to put aside the unified answers that were their unified demise and turn to the confusion of seeing the image of God within all people. Even more, the people now had the opportunity put down the tools of death that were their demise and pick up the tools of life. Though our society is full of languages, the problem is that we are stuck in the Babel of unified answers. Our only way out is to embrace the confusion and seek the life that flows out of the image of God within all people. Life is the only way to life. Killing is the wrong direction. May God confuse us out of our addiction to executions. May God save us from our unified language: *death.*

Searching for the truth
And, none was found
I looked up
And, I looked down

What was it like to leave Babel? One second you know everything, and the next second you know nothing. I bet it was magical. Can you imagine what it would be like to leave? One second you are executing people, and the next second you are caring for them. Confusion has a way of helping us lean further into the beauty of creation. Language that is confused is purer than language that is uniform. We have adopted the language of death because the language of life is too confusing. The death penalty is the clearest answer we can create. We think we have the right answer. The problem is that our answer has nothing to do with God.

The older you get, the more confusing life gets, I guess. It seems that God made it that way. From Eden to Babel, life grew more and more confusing. I think we are just emulating God. We are growing in our confusion as we grow in our understanding. Knowledge creates new frontiers. Answers create borders and boundaries that build upward in the certainty that heaven is close. Once you get to the top, you realize that "dumbassicity" is your companion. You can't build to heaven. You can only be heaven. The death penalty is similar to the Tower of Babel. We decided to kill people because we thought that killing was the answer. We've killed person after person thinking that we were one step closer to heaven. When we have the courage to stop and look around, it doesn't take long to realize that "dumbassicity" is all you've found.

Following

"...where is the lamb...?" -Genesis 22:7

Hundreds and hundreds of people have been executed over the past few decades. People don't die at that speed without everyone deciding to follow evil. Following is always the problem. The truth is that you really can't *follow* love. Love is something that you *are*. You can't follow killing in love. What in the hell does love have to do with killing? How is anyone going to love God and follow the path of killing? I guess they would have to believe that God is a killer. Sometimes, I can understand why people might assume that God is a killer. I just don't understand why they would stay there.

"Hell is the trauma of getting killed over and over." Sitting on the edge of my seat, I was overwhelmed by my professor's descriptions. The more I thought about it, the more I trembled. God was repeatedly killing people to punish them for their lives. I had never thought about it like that. Since I knew God was all about torture in other stories, I accepted the terrifying notion. It made sense in the midst of our theology of death. Hell and killing always seemed to fit. Repeatedly, I assured myself that I wasn't going there. I knew that hell was for those who don't know God. I knew God. I thought.

The music thumped. The lights bounced. We were in the middle of a performance. Everyone felt the power. We were in the show. Then, huge guys ran out to perform spectacular feats. With the crowd going crazy, I saw a guy rip a phonebook in half. With fire raging, I saw another guy punch through wood and blocks. With veins popping out of his arms, I watched a guy bend a frying pan into a burrito. From crowbars to wood to metal to fire to ice to baseball bats to nails to poles, nothing was out of bounds. We saw it all. During one of the times of devotion, we were told that we too could live out an extreme faith. With the music thumping, I wondered about all the pumped up masculinity in the room. For a moment, I felt like all the testosterone might be actually leading us *away* from God. Then, I decided to stop thinking. I remembered that I had to have faith.

Abraham heard God. I always get skeptical when I hear such words. *What does God sound like? What's the difference between a psychotic meltdown and hearing from God?* You ever had people tell you that they've heard a word from God? I've known a few. They're not the type of persons who anyone would want to be associated with. One stole money. One was a serial adulterer. One was a liar. I could go on and on. By this point, Abraham was a few of the things that I mentioned. After many years of trying with Sarah, Abraham finally had the son that God had promised him, Isaac. When you throw in all the craziness that led up to the birth of Isaac, you wouldn't blame anybody for being more than a little skeptical of various parts of Abraham's story. I don't even know if God believed everything that Abraham was throwing out there. Regardless, there is no doubt that Isaac was Abraham's favorite. Isn't that all that's supposed to matter?

I read an article about a killer on death row. I was well into seminary by this point. The killer killed multiple people in horrific ways. Throughout the trial, the prosecutor grabbed everyone's attention and wouldn't let go. Reading his words, I felt like I was there. By the time the "guilty" verdict was announced, I was happy. I didn't think that death was enough for this killer. I wanted the killer to get even more. I wanted the killer to suffer like his victims had suffered. After I released much anger, I looked down to realize that there was still many words left in the article. I couldn't believe it. Was the guilt found in the tragedy not enough? What more was there to say? It took a few words to make me realize that there was much more to say.

Can you imagine punching an infant? Can you imagine telling your child how worthless they are? Can you imagine making someone live in a closet? The stories of how the killer was abused were limitless. Just like Isaac, the killer's dad tried to kill him too. The defense attorney brought in witness after witness to emphasize the defendant's history of horrific abuse as a child. Eventually, the judge cut it off. Then, the prosecutor simply rehashed the details of the violent crime. When a sentence of death was handed down, people wondered if anybody had listened to the mitigating circumstances. Did all of these awful things that happened to the killer not count for anything? I was so angry. How could we be so cruel? How could we allow evil to perpetuate evil? There was more than enough evidence for this man to be spared death. There was more than enough evidence.

God told Abraham to sacrifice Isaac. The story is supposed to be about extreme faith. While certainly extreme, I don't think the story is about faith. This is a story of mental illness. Abraham was out of his mind. This is a man who believed God was telling him to sacrifice his own child. Can you imagine hearing God tell you to kill somebody, and then preparing to do it? I've spoken with many guys on death row who believe God told them to commit heinous crimes. I've heard stories that would make your skin crawl. What's the difference between the guys on death row and Abraham? Maybe they're the same. Perhaps, both are the victims of child abuse. Abraham was told to kill his child by a God who knew Abraham would do it. How abusive is that? Many of the people on death row are abused to the point that violence is all that they know. Does God let the abuse happen with the idea that a killer is being created? It seems that God is at the top of the abuse chain. Maybe that's where people get their ideas of abuse from. Is God just as mentally ill and abusive as the killers?

I learned about abuse early. I felt the hand. I felt the belt. I felt the switch. I felt the electrical cord. I felt the words. I felt the words the deepest. Did God give the order to abuse me? I've always wondered. Abraham favored Isaac over Ishmael. Before the command to sacrifice Isaac, one has to spend a few moments thinking about the shunning of Ishmael. Born of Abraham's wife's servant, Ishmael was sent away without any inheritance. Was Abraham a deadbeat dad? I've known many guys on death row whose parents shunned them. Deadbeat parents have a way of turning children of God into killers. God shuns so many in the old stories. How are people supposed to react when shunning is a possibility? Isaac did everything he was supposed to do. Isaac sought to live into being the child of the promise. Isaac was afraid of being shunned like Ishmael. What was Isaac thinking when he was walking to that place of sacrifice? I bet he wasn't preparing to rip a phonebook in half or bend a frying pan. Isaac's walk was about love, not toxic masculinity.

The final walk is spiritual. It doesn't matter who's being killed. There is something very meaningful about the last steps of someone's life. There was nothing spiritual about Isaac's walk to the place of sacrifice. Lunacy controlled everything. What was Abraham thinking? Final appeals are often frantically filed to keep people from being executed. Why would you walk your son to his own death? Many people argue that Abraham had extreme faith. I disagree. Like the toxic "masculinity team," I think that Abraham was so sick that he actually believed God was telling him to do all sorts of things out of the toxic masculinity playbook. Abraham was out of his mind. How else do you explain someone leading another to that person's death? We do what Abraham did all the time. We get ready to execute someone because we believe that we've heard a word from God. Are we sure it's God? Did God tell us to do it? What difference does it make? A God that goes around telling people to kill people is no God. That God is *Evil*, and *Evil* is never God. Do you believe in an *Evil* that kills, or the *real* God, who comes to bring about life? Killing and God don't mix. So, who was speaking to Abraham?

I read about a guy who killed a bunch of people because he believed that God told him to do it. The story drew me in. For many years, I learned about "God" telling people to do all sorts of strange, violent things. These stories recalled to my mind the story of when Abraham almost sacrificed Isaac. "God" told Abraham to kill his son. Who's to say that these other killers I read about didn't hear something about killing as well? The question deeply troubled me. I couldn't sleep. I couldn't eat. I kept thinking the same thoughts. If God told Abraham to kill, certainly God has told others to kill. Old stories kept rushing my brain. *Who's to say there weren't tons of people running around who heard a killer word from God? Are there people in our churches? Could there even be somebody in my own family? Maybe I'm going to get a message about killing!* When I went into the pastor's office, he was not prepared for my question. From the moment I opened my mouth, he swatted me back with condescending comments, "Your sin is what is causing you to have this brain struggle." I disagreed. I should have remembered that my pastor was useless. Then, I went to another pastor friend. We hashed it out until the early morning. Eventually, we decided God doesn't tell people to kill people. You can't love your neighbors *and* kill them. Anyone who thinks that someone is saying to kill people is very sick and deserving of our compassion. Though I was still a little unsure, I pushed into these thoughts.

"Where's the sacrifice?" Can't you hear the desperate words of Isaac get louder and louder as the place of sacrifice approaches? Abraham has no reply except to point to the God that he listened to. You can bet that Abraham was wondering about the instructions he thought he heard. Isaac was wondering too. In the moments leading up to an execution, everyone doubts. How

could you be human and not be troubled by the death of another human? I guess not everyone is troubled. There is far too much killing in our world for everyone to be troubled. I wonder if God is troubled. There seems to be far too much killing going on in our world for God to be troubled. With all of his strength, Abraham placed Isaac on the altar. The executioners placed the inmate on the gurney. Can you imagine Isaac looking up in terror? What type of God would put any of us through such a thing? Abraham remained steady. Ever devoted to what he thought God was saying, Abraham kept wondering if he had made a mistake. *What type of God would put a man through such a thing?* The executioners prepared the needle. Abraham prepared the knife. Time slowed down and crept toward the hour. Sweat poured off every brow. Terror was all that anyone knew. When the hour hit, Abraham brought the knife down as fast as he could. Isaac shrieked out in fear. Something stopped the knife. Regardless of whether it was God or not, whatever told Abraham to pull all this shit was responsible for the trauma that both father and son were facing. How could any God put two people through something like this? The time of execution arrived. The poison was injected. No one stopped the execution. Everybody thought they were doing what God told them to do. Everyone was trying to live out their extreme faith. Blood is required for killing folk. God didn't stop this execution. God doesn't stop most executions. God prefers for people to experience the trauma of killing and being killed. The executed lays dead. There was no one to save him. Is this the extreme faith we're supposed to be pushing into? There was only us and we preferred to keep our distance. Since the days of Abraham and before, we have believed in a God that abuses and traumatizes people. Why do you think we are so comfortable with killing people? We have to revolutionize our minds on a few things. The almost-sacrifice of Isaac was about extreme "dumbassicity," not extreme faith. Our death penalty is about extreme "dumbassicity," not extreme faith. "If it ain't love, it ain't God." How can a God of love be about killing? *Oh God, please heal us from this case of the "dumbass" we've contracted from listening to your dumb ass.*

You told me to follow
But, I didn't know
That you are the only one
That you love so

The sacrifice stopped. The *sacrifice* of Isaac became the *almost-sacrifice* of Isaac. Everyone lived happily ever after...right? Hardly. For the rest of his life, Isaac closed his eyes and saw his father standing over him with a knife. Can you imagine waking up or going to bed with that image every night? Death row is repeatedly like an almost-execution. Trauma is inflicted every hour of every day. The small space closes in. The trauma never leaves. There is no air. Every time you close your eyes, the trauma is there. Many of the inmates are desperate to be sacrificed, just to make the trauma stop. Believing that redemption of some sort is still possible in the land of the living, most inmates cling to life. Unlike Isaac, those who are eventually executed are silenced. But, what if they could speak? What if one of the costs of executing someone was that you had to listen to them after their death? Can you imagine hearing of the horror and pain that accompanied those final minutes? More to the point, can you imagine feeling what the executed felt? I bet we would stop executing people. Actually, we probably wouldn't. We seem to be following the path of our creator. We think that extreme faith is about servicing our addiction to death.

Genocide

"You shall annihilate them..." -Deuteronomy 20:17

"Davis didn't show no mercy to that white cop." At least in the South, race is always there. If you don't pay attention, you might miss it. But, make no mistake...race is always there. For my cousin, he couldn't get over the fact that Troy Davis was convicted of killing a white cop. Due to his racism, my cousin couldn't hear the evidence. I wondered how many other people there were like that. Davis was a black man convicted and sentenced disproportionately by a largely white judicial system in the South. Doesn't that story sound familiar? Race is always there. Persons of color are consistently sentenced to death at higher rates. In courtrooms throughout the South, the scene has been repeated. Our judicial system has perpetuated a quiet form of genocide against persons of color. The only people who seem to hear it are the ones closet to it. From mass incarceration to the death penalty, we have seen persons of color disproportionately sentenced throughout our history. Race matters in this country. Race particularly matters in the South. Those who choose to believe that race doesn't matter are guilty of the crimes their willful ignorance causes. Troy Davis is dead because of racism. In the midst of a largely white judicial system, Davis never got a fair shake. These states are only a promised land for some. Why didn't God step in? Why didn't God fix the situation? Maybe racism is deeply rooted in God.

In the book of Deuteronomy, God commands the genocide of multiple races. There were the Hittites, Amorites, Canaanites, Perizzites, Hivites, and the Jebusites—to name a few. Can you imagine if this list read the Jews, Muslims, Blacks, Immigrants, Disabled, and Homosexuals? God commanded the people to leave nothing alive. What type of God would command such a thing? Does a God of love have anything to do with a God that commands genocide? Hell no. God is not with the conquerors. God was out there with the victims. God is incarnate in those we seek to kill. God lies on the beds of death row. God is strapped to the gurney. God feels the needle.

In the midst of these of these horrific commands of genocide, it is no wonder that followers of God are so addicted to killing. The death penalty seems to fit right in. I guess everybody thinks that they're just keeping up the old family traditions. In the midst of my transition to a stronger stance against the death penalty, I remember having a conversation with a conservative theologian.

"Do you actually believe that God commands us to kill people?" I asked.

"Not only do I believe it, I want our nation to practice it," he responded.

I continued: "So, you're saying that you believe that the death penalty is a tool of God? What does that have to do with a God of love?"

"Love sometimes means that you have to kill."

I tried again. "Does God have to kill?"

"God is punishing our sin. In many ways, God is just following our lead on killing."

"I don't buy it. None of it makes sense to me. God is love. That's what I believe in."

"You are going to end up loving you some hell."

I've had this conversation a million times. People defend the death penalty by using stories of genocide and other atrocities to turn God into a monster. Let's turn our eyes to God.

Let the heads roll
Wipe them off the scrolls
God won't stop
Until the bodies drop
Don't stand in God's way
This is murder day

"You've been convicted of the killing of billions. You were not there. You never have been. You are something that we thought we needed. You are not God. You are death. For your crimes, you're punishment is death. This will be the last execution we'll ever need." The authorities didn't waste any time. God was marched to the chamber. Right before the execution, God was read the story of Creation, the almost-sacrifice of Isaac, and various other "divine" stories of atrocities and killing. Everyone was silent. "What will happen if this is the real God?" The chaplain spoke, "God cannot be killed. The real God lives in resurrection." Immediately after the chaplain's words, huge amounts of poison started pumping into God's veins. Leaning up, God screamed God's last words, "I'm sending you all to hell for this!" A little boy spoke up and said, "Because of your crazy stories and commands, we've already lived in hell." The physician stepped forward to check God's pulse. Moments passed. God was dead.

Bones

"Can these bones live?" -Ezekiel 37:3

I couldn't find God. I was there when they killed Troy Davis. I felt the spirit leave. Afraid, I wondered what happened. For hours, I stayed in that space of darkness. I knew I'd changed. I could never go back. The hour grew later and later. Time was no more. I closed my eyes. I was transported to a different place. There was a valley full of bones. I knew the bones. I saw the bones of Troy Davis and all the others who have been executed. In the midst of them all, the divine voice cried out, "Can these bones live?" I knew that voice. I'd wanted to hear it for so long. God was there. God was in the midst of the least of these. Again, the divine voice demanded, "Can these bones live?" I replied, "Oh God, you know." "Then speak love in the midst of hate." Suddenly, there was a noise. The bones started coming together. My entire body shook. How did I get here? Then, muscle wrapped around the bones. I watched in amazement. I was unable to believe my eyes. Then, flesh and skin came together. Everything was flying around in the sky. "Prophesy to the breath!" God shouted. I did as I was told. Life came back. Electricity sparked all around. Breath filled the assembled. Looking around, I saw God standing in the midst of the executed. Troy Davis was there too. I knew that I wanted to be counted in that number. I started running toward God. Before I could get there, my eyes were open and I was back in my bed. God had brought me out of my grave of ignorance. I knew that I was ready to give the rest of my life to abolition.

God was executed
God is dead
Are we finally free?

All the people said

    Behold, I saw the equipment start to move. I heard a voice declare that the execution was underway. Someone screamed.

BODIES

Behold, I saw a microphone come down from the heavens. "Do you have any final words?" God had plenty.

Words

"In the beginning was the Word..." -John 1:1

Please stop talking
Oh, let's just do some walking
Reconciliation only takes two
And right now, I'm simply desperate to hear you

Thoughts combined to form the movements that made the lines. Ideas brought the lines together to form letters. Desire brought letters together to form the Word. Pictures formed. Beauty escaped. Expression was divine. Throughout eternity, God was alone. The darkness swirled repeatedly. God leaned in. The Word was there. God could hear it. The Word brought melodies to the ears of God that was unlike anything God had ever heard.

God could feel it. The Word touched God in ways that God had never been touched. God knew it. The divine brain drowned in ecstasy. God smelled it. The aroma was intoxicating. God tasted it. The Word exploded in the mouth of God. God saw it. The Word kept going forth to transform the cosmos. The Word is a constant interactive expression of God. The Word was God and God was the Word. We encounter the Word when the Word wells up within us and touches us. The Word exists when the image of God is born with the Words. We are the Words. We are the presence of God in the land of the living.

Inmates on death row live in a world of darkness. Solitary confinement is standard practice in many states. For most inmates, the only touch that they ever feel is when the guard places handcuffs on their wrists. Noises visit from time to time. In the midst of it all, it's hard to know what is real or not. Everyone is desperate for something that's real. In the darkness, many inmates pray for the Word. Looking out the small window, many inmates search for the Word. Hugging their bodies, many inmates seek to feel the Word. Reading religious texts, many inmates seek to know the Word. After something has been cooked, many inmates seek to smell the Word. Sometimes the Word comes. Sometimes the Word seems lost. Sometimes the Word is missed. It still feels like there is a Word out there somewhere. Can the Word pierce the darkness? Can the Word make it into such a small cell? Where can one find the Word in the midst of isolation? What will the Word look like? The Word comes through the bars. "You've got a letter." Who knew that the Word could be delivered? *In the beginning...*

In the midst of various formulations of modernity, it seems that we've lost each other. There was a time when friends looked at each other. Now, we have social media, where nobody knows whether anybody is real or not. Do you remember a time when love was spoken more than it was typed? Neighbors don't know each other. Common spaces of physical interaction are quickly disappearing. Our dehumanizing trajectory only increases our ability to dehumanize those around us. I think this has only increased our ability to ignore executions. Real love seems old fashioned in times like these. I couldn't ignore what was going on, I needed to respond. After a pastor told me about a spiritual group that was facilitating relationships with people on death row, I knew I was hearing *the* Word of God.

There is nothing overwhelming about the website. The logo is of a letter passing through bars. Even the name "Death Row Support Project" is not all that sexy. The organization is a very simple outfit. After I contacted the group about writing to someone on death row, I received a letter in the mail with a letter from an inmate requesting a pen pal and instructions. Like with most things, I dove right in. Before I knew it, John and I were becoming friends. I decided to visit. For a few hours, John told me in precise detail how he was framed for his crimes. The stories got wilder and wilder as the visit continued. I didn't know anything. I intentionally didn't research anything about his case until after I talked to him about it. On the drive home, I was struck by the way that John made me feel. The dark parts of his eyes seemed to stare right through me. The tattoos looked so evil. If he had the chance, I felt like he would've killed me right then and there. On the drive home, I meditated on everything that happened. I prayed that God would show me what to do. I heard God tell me to keep at it. When I got home and opened up a graphic letter that John had earlier mailed to my wife, I knew God was wrong. My wife concurred. Even in the midst of all the craziness, I did feel like John shared one powerful piece of the Word with me: "Jeff, you have to be careful who you trust." The good folks at the Death Row Support Project apologized profusely and sent me another letter.

Paper
Words
Letters
Life
You need to be careful
Of that man with a knife

From the moment I opened the letter, I knew Dominique was a hustler. In paragraph two, Dominique asked me to send him $200. In paragraph three, Dominique described an organization that he needed me to set up immediately. In paragraph four,

Dominique told me to pick up his girl and bring her down to visit. The demands continued for pages. I felt like I was reading a ransom note. The problem was that I didn't know what was being held hostage. I felt like I would find out. When I finally decided to write, I didn't really know what to say. Should I respond to all of Dominique's demands? I'd never even interacted with this guy before. I decided to write a letter of introduction. Less than a week later, I received a note inviting me down for a visit. I knew that God was in prison and I felt called to visit. Would hear a word from God? The first words I heard were, "Why didn't you do everything I asked you to do?" Dominique berated me for multiple hours. The demands were the only thing on his mind. In the midst of the visit, Dominique shared the day's Word: "God is like me...just even more demanding." I knew he was right. After a few more letters, I realized I just wasn't responsive enough to his demands. The Word was out there somewhere. The Death Row Support Project never stopped helping or apologizing. "Working with guys on death row is tough. Sometimes, there are no perfect matches." After a few days, another letter arrived in the mail.

Letters circled around in my head. They wanted to pull together, but they couldn't. There were too many obstacles. The Word was lost. I knew that I wanted to connect with people on death row. I just didn't know how. After two attempts, I was no closer to a friendship with someone on death row than I was when I started. I felt like a total failure. I wondered if God felt the same way. God actually lives on death row. I could still hear God calling. The letters started to come together. Something grabbed my soul. Could the Word be real?

After a few pleasantries, Chuck got down to business. "I'm lonely. I'm hurting. I'm angry. I just need someone to talk to." The letters started running into each other. I couldn't keep them straight.

"Was this just a bunch of bullshit?" I asked the question repeatedly. I didn't want to get used again. I didn't want to feel abused again. I just wanted to experience God. The letters raced. I finally grabbed my head. I closed my eyes. After a couple of deep breathes, I was able to put the demons to bed long enough to write a response. Pushing through, I pretty much said, "I'm here for you." I didn't say anything about my family. I'd already been down that road before. I didn't offer any commitments. I didn't make any offers about what I could do to help on his case. I didn't offer any money. I just offered myself. Relieved, I sealed the letter. I felt like my soul was placed inside. I licked the stamp. Something about it tasted more bitter than usual. I figured that the Word sometimes has a bitter taste to it. I didn't hold my nose. I wanted to take it all in. The letters started pushing past the obstacles. Things started shaking loose. I felt like God was there. After a couple of weeks, I knew that letter was a waste of time. Nothing arrived in the mail. I put so much emotion into all of this ridiculousness. With a fist raised to heaven, I cursed God. "Why did you push me to do this shit? Fuck the Word!" Somehow I was placed right in front of the mailbox, I opened the door. Right on top, there was an envelope from Chuck. I didn't expect to be so overwhelmed at the sight of a letter. After reading a few lines, the letters started crashing into each other. I could feel them coming together. They touched me. The mind opened. The skies burst forth. The light radiated. The miraculous happened. The letters stuck together. I could see it. I could hear it. I could know it. The Word became flesh and dwelt amongst us...

I'm stuck on death row.
Don't you know
God is here too
And we love you so

Facilitating spiritual connection after spiritual connection, the Death Row Support Project continues to do the work of God in the land of the living. God dwells within the least of these. God dwells in prison. God dwells on death row. God is in each of these letters. The letters contain the letters that come together to bring us the Word made flesh. While not always perfect, the Word finds us in the midst of such communication. Chuck and I have now been friends for years. I serve as his spiritual advisor. If Chuck is executed, I will be one of the last persons to be with him. The letters keep coming. Though our letters eventually turned into regular visits, the letters keep coming together to form the Word. When we're together, the letters bond and the Word becomes flesh. "How are you connected to the letters? The letters make up the Word. You can't expect to meet the Word without the letters. I guess you have to start somewhere." In the midst of a guided conversation about the death penalty at a conservative church, I talked about Chuck. Everyone in the crowd leaned forward and was fascinated by the idea of having a friendship with someone on death row. "God knows no boundaries!" When I told the people that Chuck was Jewish, a lady piped up and said, "Forget death row; how can you be the spiritual guide of someone who is Jewish?" Slowly looking up, I replied, "What a funny question; I've had an amazing relationship with a Jewish guy named Jesus for most of my life." The devastation of the death penalty knows no boundaries. The presence of God doesn't either.

Wine

"Fill the jars with water." -John 2:7

This wedding water
Tastes a little hotter
Than, I ever imagined
That, a liquid ever could

Water is at the center of it all. *Humanity?* Water. *Our planet?* Water. *Me?* Water. *You?* Water. Right after I found out about this, I remember staring at the water in the bottom of the toilet. I couldn't believe the water that was catching my urine was the same water that makes up our existence. Well, I guess it's not *exactly* the same water. Nevertheless, I started thinking about water all the time. Have you ever thought about turning into water? You know, reverting back to our nature? We would just become "waterpeople." Every day would be a "splash." Even though I'm made up of water, I don't really like getting wet. I guess I'm water-adverse at times. Water is out there. Water is here. Water is in us. God loves water. All you have to do is look around. Way up top, God is taking the running plunge on the waterslide. As the waves crash, God dives continuously into the salty foam. Over there, God is splashing around in the tub. Down below, God dives deeper and deeper. Even more than that, God *is* water. God is in us. God is around us. God is before us. God is beyond us. God cycles. God is the mist. God is the rain. God is the clouds. God is the ice. God is water. God is. Just as God inhabits the most ordinary of people, God has chosen the most ordinary of elements to work many miracles.

How many weddings have you been to? I've been to a bunch. Most of the weddings were tremendous fun. I've officiated a bunch of them. Regardless of my role in the ceremony, I love dancing the night away with my wife. While we're not experts, we have a good time. I guess you could say that we follow each other's lead. Life is like that sometimes. I certainly experience it with the guys I work with on death row. Every first meeting on death row is like dancing at a wedding. Regardless of the pace of the music, we just try to listen to each other and follow each other's lead. I wonder if Jesus danced that night in Cana? I wonder if Jesus was simply following the lead of the others?

My fingers tightly gripped the wheel. Thoughts of destiny ran through my head. Legs shaking. I held the letter in my hand. Why did I even have the letter with me? They weren't going to check when I arrived. Mile after mile passed by. I felt like the end was coming at any moment. *Maybe this is the way the guys felt on the last walk?* I wondered about life and death. Life seemed so trivial in the face of death. *Who cares what gas station I pulled into? Do people on death row ever get to make an actual choice? What about my life?* I knew that I was heading to a place of no return. Death wouldn't be much further down the highway. When I turned off the highway, I thought I was going to puke. I was experiencing a whirlwind of emotions. Pulling from every direction, I finally got it together. Driving past the building where people are actually executed, I struggled to keep from crying. I felt like I was losing it. Straightening up, I kept on driving. These were the last miles that any inmate about to be executed would see. Life is beautiful. Lakes fill the path. The different colors from the sky and the deep connect to form magical tapestries unbelievable hues. The water reminded me that God was near. When I turned off on the last road, I was okay. There were a few more pastures and random houses to see before I arrived. "Stop!" I applied the brakes hard and my old car grinded to a halt. "License. Open the hood. Open the trunk. Open all the doors. Step back." I was a little taken aback by it all. I felt like a criminal. In this place, I guess everybody does. On the far stretch, most people don't even come out alive. I trembled. The trunk slammed. I didn't know what was next. "Are you going to get back in your car? Park in space 8!" Even after I parked, I didn't know where to go. The barbed wire fences were ominous. What did that siren mean? Eventually, I followed everyone else. "Remove everything from your pockets. Take off your shoes. Walk through. Go back! What's in your pocket?" I forgot the quarter. Pulling out the shiny quarter, I handed it to the officer. "Driver's license. Who you here to see? Okay. I got you. Go on through." The door slammed louder than any door I'd ever heard. Sweat poured off me. My armpits felt like swamps. My chest felt like a slip and slide. Everything grew moist at the same time. Even my socks were wet. When I walked through the next door, I almost turned around. The door slammed. There was one more barbed wire gate. I couldn't figure out how to open it. From the heavens, a voice cried out, "PUSH!" I started walking to the next door. Prisoners called out to me from their cells. I was in the belly of the beast. I had to push my legs to keep going. Based on the struggles I was feeling, God must not have made it through the metal detector. The next door opened and quickly closed. I kept pushing. *What's that smell?* I wondered. I don't know if the smell or the cold was worse. Both combined to make the experience very unpleasant. I didn't have time to stop and smell the roses...or shit. I had a booth to find. The last two doors were difficult. "Who are you?" I showed my badge. "Stand there!" The door opened. I didn't move. I tried to listen. "Go!" I was scared. I'd never been through anything like this before. Once in the room, I had no idea where to go. "Sir! Are you here for a visit?" "I am." "Who are you here to visit?" I walked halfway down the booths and entered the bathroom. Water slowly leaked out of the faucet. After flushing my breakfast down the toilet, I walked out. The person in front of me pointed to the booth. Our eyes met. I picked up the phone. This would be the first miracle: *Water meeting in hopes of transforming into wine.* I've experienced this moment many times since. There is one time that I'll never forget.

The conversation was strange from the first words. He began: "How are you doing, young man?" The words bounced around my head. Even though I'd already sent him multiple letters, I could tell that he had forgotten who I was. Question jumped over question before I was able to explain. Honestly, it's hard to explain anything when questions are flying at you. "I'm Rev. Hood. Remember?" As if he was coming in from somewhere else, Stacey bounced back. "Of course, I know who you are! I just lost my thoughts for a minute." I had my doubts. We continued talking. Stacey came in and out. Despite the confusion, Stacey kept smiling and talking. "Do you like clowns? I can draw any kind of clown you want. Ever since I was a child, I've just loved clowns..." We stayed on Stacey's favorite subject for a considerable amount of time. Even though it was obvious that Stacey had severe mental disabilities, I'd never heard any human talk about clowns so much. "I love the big shoes. I love the white faces. I love the suspenders. Those clowns are always sneaking up on you and pulling the craziest tricks. Clowns know how to do things that other people don't. They're magic!" Just as I was sensing that the conversation was moving beyond clowns, Stacey started to talk about raping and murdering his girlfriend's 2-year-old child. Though the descriptions were often imprecise, I didn't question what he was talking about. I felt like I was listening to a confession. After hearing Stacey's initial thoughts, I put the phone down and leaned back in my chair. I was overwhelmed. I wanted to leave. I prayed, "God, I'm trusting you've sent me here for a reason." I prayed. I stayed. One of the traditions of death row is for visitors to buy snacks out of the vending machines for the inmates. I think I picked up a couple of sodas and some snack cakes. Once Stacey's soda and snack cake were placed in a bag and handed to the guard, I watched her hand the bag off to other guards, who delivered them to Stacey. Even though we were on death row, there was a tremendous amount of service taking place. Once the food arrived, I prayed again. The water in the soda turned into wine. The snack cakes turned into the body of God. Stacey's spirit was refreshed. He stopped talking about clowns for a few moments. *Did God show up?* Knowing that this might be my last visit, I offered a long prayer for Stacey. "Please help him get his mind right." After the first few words, I realized that mental improvement would get him executed faster. So I tried again. "Please keep him from being executed." I think Stacey's last words were about clowns.

Water is used for all sorts of things at a wedding. People wash their hands before the event. Everyone wants to be clean for such a magical event. Think about how many people bathed before the wedding at Cana. The animals were drinking out of the water. Thirst is not limited to a particular species. Flies were dying in the water. I guess death isn't limited to any particular species, either. All of the pots and pans were scrubbed in the water. Who knows what was stuck to the sides of the vessels? In the midst of all of the excitement, no one would want to miss their turn to defecate. I'm sure everyone would need a good splash in their ass to clean things up after the feast. You know how everybody always goes to the bathroom before the movie starts? Everyone would need to use water before, after, and during an event like this. This is why they had so much of it. When Jesus turned the water into wine, the scriptures don't say anything about the water being clean.

Tim invited me into a world of violence. Words became fists. Bludgeoned to the ground, Tim was never able get back up. Tears and hate flowed freely. How does someone turn out like this? The answer always lies in the beginning. Physical growth was never accompanied by maturity. The older Tim got, the more Tim got left behind. Willing to do anything to maintain relationships, Tim started drowning in trouble that only seemed to grow by the hour. The violence birthed in the beginning only seemed to grow. Screens delivered ideas. On that fateful day, the ideas took over. "Will you kill my Dad?" the computer screen blinked. Killing seemed like it wouldn't be that big of a deal. Gun in hand, Tim walked up to the door. The darkness covered everything. Terrified that he would wake up, Tim placed the gun toward the man's head and pulled the trigger. Blood sprayed. Tim got away, but not for long. Later, Tim was sentenced to a jail sentence that still allowed him a chance at freedom. The judge knew that he was only 16.

However, in prison, communion was found with the worst of the worst. There was no water. There was no wine. There was only evil.

I got death in me
And, it won't let me free
Everyday, it just keeps coming for me

Murder struck again. A fellow prisoner was strangled to death. Though Tim said he didn't do anything, the courts said that he did. Tim never thought he would get the death penalty. After gasps in the courtroom, Tim was taken away. Some just sat like it was routine. Death is a way of life here. Before long, Tim was in transport. The biggest door of them all slammed behind. Tim was in the small room that he would call home for the rest of his natural life. Though there were appeals, Tim tried not to worry about them too much. Hope wasn't worth holding on to. Tim remains one of the biggest men I've ever seen. The entire booth rocked when he sat down. We picked up our phones. The conversations carried us for hours. Though we were of mixed faiths, we both longed for deeper communion. The guard brought the "water and bread" to Tim. After some prayer, I leaned against the glass and declared, "This is the body of Jesus, murdered for you. This is the blood of Jesus, poured out for you." In the midst of the dungeon, we found God. The water turned to wine. We were set free. Though a huge glass wall separated us, I know I walked out of there with a few wine stains on my shirt.

Though you can call it whatever you want, love brought everyone together. The wedding proceeded. In those moments, everyone becomes one. Time is suspended. Love is all there is. These experiences don't come easy. Our distractions are always bigger than our ability to focus on fullness. Scared that the cohesion might break, Jesus went to get the wine. In the midst of my visits, I want love to bring us together. Sometimes it does. Sometimes it doesn't. Regardless, I'm always reaching for the wine. I don't want whatever love there is to break. I'm focused on fullness. I'm focused on restoration. I'm focused on seeing the prison as the place where God turns water into wine. Can't the celebration of love transform our minds anywhere? Isn't love what sets us free? Glass cannot hold love back. Death cannot hold love back. Bars cannot hold love back. Go to prison. Go to the wedding feast. Go to those whom society has shunned. Don't be afraid, God just started turning soda into wine.

Slices

"I want you to give me...the head of John the Baptist..."
-Mark 6:25

The blood starts to pour
Let, it hit the floor
Another, killing is going down
This is murder town

Slowly picking up the severed head, the warrior screamed in triumph. A bloody mess falls from the bottom. I feel like I've seen it a million times in the movies. Perhaps, that's where I get this image of John the Baptist's beheading from. I see a big soldier slicing the head off and delivering it to Herod with all the bloody mess falling out. I wonder how John reacted to seeing the sword? Maybe John went prayerfully. Maybe John resisted. Maybe John orchestrated some mixture. I don't think John thought he was going to die. Imagine John trying to grab the sword and getting his hand sliced off. What would it have been like for John to cling to the bars? Did John scream like a child? Did John feel abandoned by God? I bet there was no God in those moments. How could there be? God was being executed. John knew it was the end when the sword sliced his neck. Jesus apparently ignored what was happening. How can we trust anyone who could have stopped an execution and chose not to? Would you stop the execution of your own cousin? It didn't take John long to die. Even if the sword got caught on the spine and the executioner had to take two swipes, a botched execution is still usually a quick execution. Or is it? Executions are never painless or perfect. These spectacles are always botched. The execution of John the Baptist should have taught us better. Why didn't we listen? I wish that Jesus had told us to listen. I bet anyone could have heard the sounds of the breaking hearts. Even Herod was disturbed. Do you know any Herods that preside over executions? We call them governors these days. Maybe the execution of the story hits a little too close to home.

Disciples throughout the land felt the beheading of John the Baptist. Now everyone knew that they could be next. Jesus offered no comfort. Everyone just kept going—though, I would imagine that there were less people who "just kept going" after the beheading. Most followers don't want to follow all the way to the sword. While I'm sure there were whispers in the streets, I bet nobody wanted to talk openly about the beheading. What was it like to be at the party? Can you imagine gnawing on a turkey leg and seeing a dripping head come out on a platter? What if you didn't know what was going on and the head was unveiled right next to you? Did the workers stop working? I've always thought about the people at the party. What did people do when that head came out? Truthfully, I bet the party didn't stop. Everyone probably just acted as if nothing had happened. Repeatedly, no one stops when people are executed. Most of the time, no one even notices. Killing is just a part of the party.

I only met Juan Garcia once. I was asked to visit him. For a couple of hours in a cold room in Livingston, Texas, we talked. With an unforgiving deadline approaching fast, the last things were at the forefront of our minds. For most people, eschatology or the study of destiny is a theoretical conversation. When one a person is scheduled to be executed, you're not all that concerned with the theoretical. "Do you think I'm going to die?" The question was the toughest I'd ever encountered. Despite the fact that I knew the answer, I had to name it. "I cannot imagine a circumstance in which you won't be executed." Though I felt like my response was cold, the words loosened Juan up. We began our journey back to the future.

The stories of persons on death row always begin far before the murders. Drugs and abuse are common elements. In a short period of time, Juan tried to tell me all that he could. On multiple occasions, I got lost in the intensity of it all. When Juan expressed his regret over the murder, I looked him straight in the eye and said, "You're forgiven."

"What is salvation?" I don't think about the definition of salvation too often... I'm too busy living it. Nevertheless, I blurted out what came to my mind first, "We are saved when we place our faith in love." Since God is love, I have always believed that love is our only way of knowing the divine. Juan responded: "I choose love." Even as time has put distance between us, Juan's answer festers in my soul.

The last topic was one we all think about...whether we admit it or not. "What will the judgment be like?" Growing up, I was always terrified of death. Our pastors constantly talked about fire and damnation. I was never able to shake the belief that the flames were for me. When I accepted the call to ministry, I promised God I would never talk like that. I haven't. After a quick silent prayer, I leaned in and declared, "Imagine encountering a love so powerful that it burns up all the evil within you and transforms all the love within you into something eternal." Juan's eyes started to water up. *"I believe."* In the power of that moment, I knew that I did too.

Knowing that our time was coming to a close, I didn't know how to say goodbye for the first, and last, time. In the agony of trying to think of the right words to say, I was paralyzed. Sensing my timidity, Juan smiled and said, *"I think I know what will draw us together again."* Our shared faith in love remains.

A few weeks later, I stared at Juan Garcia's picture. The watch on my wrist counted down every second. *Why was I standing here?* With every tick, I knew that a beautiful person was about to be killed. I had on a white robe with a red stole. I was helping lead a protest against the death penalty in another state. *Why wasn't I there?* There was work everywhere. I wanted to be in that room. I knew that I couldn't. Trembling, I closed my eyes. I envisioned Juan on the gurney. Arm out. Needle in. Poison pumping through the line. I could hear Juan's statements of love. Then, the eyes closed in the midst of the weeping. I was back. I was protesting. My phone revealed that Juan had recently been pronounced dead.

So Long, Juan
I'll See You Again
Heaven Sure is Better
Than the Shithole You Were In

John the Baptist was senselessly executed. Is there ever an execution that's not senseless? I lost a friend. *Why?* Juan was dead. The body was delivered to a viewing area for all to see. The party kept going. Nobody stopped eating. Nobody stopped dancing. Nobody stopped working. The mechanisms of death kept turning. The party didn't stop.

A Platter Full of Head
An Execution for the Dead

The death penalty helps us to realize that life is a party only for some. Herod's friends were among the most privileged people in their society. The people in the dungeon with John the Baptist weren't. Those who run our systems of justice are usually among the most privileged people in our society. People on death row are not. Those with capital usually don't get capital punishment. Poor people occupy the spaces of death row. In addition, persons of color, immigrants, and the mentally disabled are all disproportionately represented on death row.

While I could share a bunch of statistics to prove these claims, I'd ask that you verify them with your own observations of oppression going on all around you. The folks on death row are the folks who got left out of the party. These are the folks who the party put down. These are the folks who the party ignored. When their executions happened, the party didn't care.

Jesus encouraged John the Baptist to love all people. Herod and John had a friendly relationship. The cost of loving Herod was death. There are many toxic people on death row. You can't save everybody. Sometimes your job is to catch a small glimpse of humanity and declare it to be God. When evil seems to rage so powerfully within the body of the killer in front of you, never turn away. Though the bones may rattle, God does not. Sometimes we have to meet death in order to know how to argue for life.

I will never forget those eyes. Darkness engulfed the entire pupil. I was scared before I ever sat down. While I'd occasionally had moments of struggle with my ministry on death row, I'd never experienced this strong of a desire to turn around and run as fast as I could. I didn't. I sat down and reached for the phone.

While I've never published this type of damning report about someone who is about to be executed before, I think this case calls for it. I believe that Richard Masterson is beyond mentally incompetent. I can think of few things more cruel or unusual than to execute someone who is out of his mind. Tonight, the State of Texas will try to do just that. I will be standing outside the Huntsville Unit in protest. Below, are memories of my last visit with Masterson in October that I recorded and submitted to the Board of Pardons and Paroles to try to help save his life…

On October 15, 2015, I walked to a booth about halfway down the middle row in the visitation room at the Polunsky Unit and sat. For a few minutes, I waited in prayer. I opened my eyes when I heard the door clank. Looking up, my eyes beheld a man who looked out of his mind. From his wildly dilated pupils to the strange contortions of his face, I knew something wasn't right. When I picked up the phone, Richard Masterson began to rage. I've never had that level of anger directed at me before. Over and over, Masterson told me, "I'm not gay!" I didn't care. I still don't understand why he felt the need to keep telling me that. For almost two hours, I felt the conversation grow crazier and crazier. It took all the spiritual energy I had to not get up and leave.

Masterson repeatedly told me that he wanted to die. Then, he switched gears rapidly and told me that he had a girlfriend that made him want to live. The more Masterson talked, the more confused I got. Statement after statement seemed to contradict the last. When I asked if he liked any of the guards or anyone he was housed with, Masterson told me that he wished he could kill a few of them "with his bare hands." He also pointed to the outside to assure me that there were people out there he would like to kill too. When I asked him why he would say such things when he knew he was being recorded, he shrugged and replied that he didn't give a shit.

When I told Masterson that I was a minister, he proceeded to tell me about his attraction to transgender women. Repeatedly, Masterson told me, "There ain't no pussy like a brand new pussy." I heard more explicit stories about "new pussies" than I ever wanted to hear in my entire life. Then, Masterson assured me again that he wasn't gay. When I asked about the transgender woman he was convicted of strangling to death, Masterson got really belligerent and told me, "I ain't scared to strangle nobody." Then, he told me again that he wasn't gay. If he said that he wasn't gay once, I bet he said it at least ten or eleven times. Though I managed to take a picture with Masterson, he acted paranoid about that as well. From the words that he said to the way that his body looked, Richard Masterson repeatedly proved to me that he was out of his mind.

Throughout the conversation, Masterson kept exhibiting a mix of rage and psychosis. The words that did make sense were strangely combative. The rest I found nuts. As someone who has ministered to numerous people struggling with all types of mental conditions, I have no question that Richard Masterson is not in his right mind and probably never was. Judging from my visit, I believe it would be cruel and unusual to execute Masterson.

We have to find ways to love in the midst of evil. In the midst of the near constant violence that Richard Masterson shared with me, I had to protect myself. I felt like I was under attack. Evil grabbed at my soul. There was no one to help. I went into the prison to find God. Where was anything divine now? Slowly, I realized that my present job was to report to those who were trying to save Masterson's life that I'd never seen this level of evil in someone who wasn't insane. I did. I faced evil and found love. When Masterson was executed, I stood outside the facility in protest. Killing is evil no matter who does the killing.

Masterson is gone
He didn't have to be
He was an evil person
Just like you and me

Everyone partied until Herod said to stop. When the celebration was over, people went home to puke. The excess piled up. You can't party without consequences. We shouldn't ignore what was going on. We should stop. Executions should be over. Until they are, we should be puking in disgust. The evil keeps pilling up. Our protests should too. We can't ignore the tragedy of our present circumstances. It is time to walk out the door of killing and never turn back.

The Woman

"Whoever is without sin can cast the first stone..." -John 8:7 (paraphrased)

Stop right now, all of this foolish killin'
Look over there, God's experienced the healin'

Executions are always staged events. From beginning to end, the events are orchestrated. One doesn't get executed for killing. One gets executed for what happens before and after the killing. Punishments of death have always been based on the desires of the punishers. Jesus knew.

The Pharisees noticed the woman. One of them approached her in the street. Those familiar with the tactics of the Pharisees knew what was going on. Lies and threats led to sex. Before long, the Pharisee was having sex with her. There was no love involved. There was only abuse. While everyone knew she was married, nobody cared. Desire was all that mattered. The Pharisee just kept having sex. Everything was going according to plan until the woman threatened to stop sleeping with the Pharisee. So the Pharisee called in his buddies and they hatched a plan. Everyone pretended to catch her in adultery when she was sleeping with the Pharisee. The woman didn't get caught in adultery. The woman was abused. This gave the Pharisees the room they needed to execute her. Whatever happened to the Pharisee? I would imagine that he was one of the ones pushing hardest for her execution. Under the law, adultery was punishable by death. They thought they figured out how to shut her up. Though the reasons driving an execution vary, they are always staged events. Just ask Jesus.

The Pharisees made a big show out of the arrest. Parading the woman through the streets, the Pharisees screamed out her crime. Everyone called for her death. The news loved the scene. There is something about seeing evil that gets everyone excited. I guess they are seeing the scapegoat for the first time. Regardless, the parade continued. Excitement for the execution grew with every step. When the crowd arrived at the space, Jesus was standing right in the middle. After collecting rocks for the stoning, the Pharisees threw the woman at the feet of Jesus. As the dust rose, Jesus looked up. Describing her crime, the Pharisees shouted for her execution. The entire state started to chant, "Execute her! Execute her!" Leaning in, everyone knew that Jesus was stuck. How could Jesus break the law? Instead of responding, Jesus placed his body down in the dirt with the woman and faced the rocks. If the woman was going to die, so too was Jesus. After a few challenging comments, the Pharisees walked away. Our bodies make a difference. They're the only thing that ever has.

Scott Panetti was out of his mind. For years, I'd heard about it. From his claims of being Elvis to his different personalities to representing himself at court in a cowboy outfit, there were all sorts of stories floating around. For years, people wrote letters to the government and tried to advocate on behalf of Panetti. How could any population be so desperate to execute someone who was so clearly out of his mind? When I finally encountered him from a distance, I knew that all the stories were true. I could see him jumping around, shaking his head and looking out of his mind. Turning around, I encountered a woman in platform shoes. Realizing it was Panetti's sister, I introduced myself. We spoke for a few minutes. I tried to share whatever knowledge I had. I told her that I was praying for Panetti to get a stay. Before I knew it, our time was up. I looked back at Panetti one more time. They were about to come get him. I knew I had to do something more. I responded in the most substantial way that I knew how...offering my body.

Has your church ever executed someone? Don't be appalled by such a question. Think deeper. Perhaps you've never hung someone on the cross at the front of your sanctuary, but have you considered the consequences of your inaction? Think about all the times your church could have done something to save a life and didn't. Can't think of any?

Christians are the United States' largest religious population. We execute people at one of the highest rates in the world. With Christians comprising a stunning majority of people who live here, there is no ability to blame these executions on any other faith except my own. Christians are killing people.

From the police to the judges to the politicians to the jurors to the prison guards to a whole host of others, the majority of those directly involved in the process of executing someone are actually Christians. In light of this fact, I have worked over the last few years to get churches organized and talking about abolishing the death penalty. I ask the same question every time, "Would you be interested in hosting a conversation about the death penalty?" More often than not, I hear the same response, "That is too political for our congregation." When a mass movement of Christians could quickly stop the death penalty, silence remains the primary tool of execution.

We are scheduled to execute Scott Panetti on December 3. Christians will be his primary killers. The barbarism of our crime is exacerbated by the fact that Panetti has suffered from documented mental illness for over 30 years. From being institutionalized over and over again to being classified as disabled by the Social Security Administration to shooting his in-laws to death to dressing up as a cowboy to represent his self at trial to now thinking that he is being executed for preaching and proselytizing, Panetti is very sick. In Matthew 25, there was a man named Jesus from Nazareth who was also very sick and said that we would be judged by how we treat the sick. With just a short time to go before such an injustice is carried out, one would expect the noise coming from our churches to be deafening. The truth be known, most churches don't even know that an execution is about to be carried out. When did we stop caring about the least of these? When did we stop talking about loving our neighbors as our self? When did we become killer Christians?

Just the other day, I drove by an old country church with a sign out front that read, "The Judgment is Upon Us." I know this to be true. We cannot continue to execute God's children and expect the results to be positive for the future of our people. On December 2, I will start a vigil outside the execution chamber in Huntsville, Texas. During the vigil, I will pray that we will be a people who will turn from our wicked ways, spare the life of Scott Panetti, and call upon God to heal our land. In this most holy time of year, I ask that you join me.

Driving fast, I pushed into the coolness of the evening. Driving through the same terrain that anyone being executed would see on their final ride, I prayed that Scott Panetti would never see any of this until he was free. The mind considers many different forms of freedom when thinking about executions. On this drive, I was only thinking about saving his life. My car didn't have any heat. I was freezing. Regardless, I knew what I had to do. When I arrived in town, I got some chips and a drink. I knew that I would need them later. I got the 10-foot tall cross out of the trunk. After I got it up in the air, I stood there for a moment. A chill ran down my spine. I was alone. I started praying. I didn't stop. Prison guards kept walking by. Even though most were laughing, one guard stopped to quietly tell me that she was opposed to the death penalty and was particularly opposed to the execution of Panetti. Before much longer, the warden came out and declared, "What are you doing out here? Don't you know that the execution isn't for a few more days?" "Sir, I'll be out here standing vigil until they stop it." "O-kay. That's your right." The temperature continued to drop. I froze. I prayed. I checked for updates. Just when I thought I wouldn't be able to stand out there any longer, I got word, "The execution of Scott Panetti has been called off." The body worked.

Prayer felt more powerful than ever. Panetti wasn't going to die. The executioners walked away. I did too.

They didn't
Get him tonight
Ol' Panetti
Put up one hell of a fight
Everyone
Get down to pray
Let's get Ol' Panetti
A permanent stay

Imagine trying to execute someone. Instead of mourning the victim, you want one more. In the public square, you want more blood. At trial, you demand another body. Once the sentence is pronounced, you celebrate another tragedy. Between the sentence and the execution date, you push for the end of the life of another. When the time comes, you get really excited. You are ready for the execution until bodies start getting between you and the condemned. The bodies are the family of the condemned. The bodies are the people who've gotten to know the condemned. The bodies are the activists giving their lives for the condemned. As you get more and more confused, you realize that there is one body that seems to stand out amongst the crowd. "Let anyone among you who is without sin be the first to throw a stone..."

Dead Man Walking

"Lazarus, come out!" -John 11:43

That guy was supposed to die
Now, I can't believe my eyes
It wasn't supposed to happen anything like this

Sickness used to come upon folks quickly. I guess it still does. One of those sicknesses got hold of Lazarus and killed him. Jesus was so depressed. For multiple years, the two shared deep love. Eventually, Jesus got to the place where Lazarus lay dead. After shedding a few tears, Jesus went to work. Everyone knew how much Jesus loved him. "Open up the tomb!" Nobody wanted to engage the dead body. Finally, Jesus commanded, "Lazarus, come out!" To the shock of everyone there, Lazarus got up and walked out. Jesus ordered them, "Unbind him, and let him go."

Joseph Rudolph Wood III gasped for almost two hours before he died. Arizona didn't know what they were doing. Dennis McGuire gasped for almost twenty-five minutes before he died. Ohio didn't know what they were doing. Clayton Lockett died of a heart attack after the procedure was stopped. Oklahoma didn't know what they were doing. Michael Wilson felt his whole body burn. Once *again*, Oklahoma didn't know what they were doing. Brian Keith Terrell was poked for over an hour. Georgia didn't know what they were doing. Brandon Jones had his eyes wide open after over half an hour of prodding. Georgia *still* didn't know what they were doing. Botched executions are becoming more and more common as states struggle to figure out how to execute people with dwindling supplies. Companies have realized it is bad for business when their drug is known for killing and not saving. Executions are always botched. There isn't a damn thing routine about killing somebody. however, these executions were *really* botched. These states created a situation of torture. In great pain, the condemned lingered between life and death for a considerable amount of time. During that time, I bet they met Lazarus. There wouldn't have been much time to talk. Lazarus was racing to get back to the land of the living. With other things on their minds, the condemned race toward glory.

This was the hour. There was nothing Rommell Broom could do. All the appeals had failed. The gurney was all that was left. Terrified, Broom pushed on. Once everything was set up, the executioners went to work finding a vein. For over two hours, executioners poked Broom with needles. Nothing worked. As the spectacle continued, Broom cried, shook, rocked and grabbed his face. Officials eventually halted the execution. Broom had survived the torture. Lazarus survived too. Suspended somewhere between life and death, Lazarus was called back. When I first heard about Broom's close encounter with death, I couldn't think of anybody but Lazarus. For those who say that Lazarus wasn't guilty of crimes, I simply say that we don't know that. The experiences of Lazarus are closer to Broom's experiences than ours are. Maybe Lazarus was looking out for Broom for some reason and pulled him out of the execution chamber. I don't know what happened. I just know that God looked down and said, "Rommell, come out."

Needles.
More needles.
We have to get this done.
We are the killers and he is the one.

Lazarus survived. Most people on death row don't. People on the outside of the tomb just stand there with fake tears in their eyes. People are dying and people just pretend to care. People mourn to be polite. Sometimes people let go and unleash their true feelings. There is nothing more disgusting than celebrating the death of another. People tried to kill Rommell Broom and people will try to kill again. People can't seem to remember that you can't love your neighbors while killing them. Who would want to be loved like that? God is standing at the tomb of killing that we all inhabit through our connections to this execution system. We don't realize how much executions are killing us. We can't survive. Lazarus is pointing us towards life. We are choking on our failure to move. God is shouting out, "Get out of that tomb!"

The Final Hours

"I am deeply grieved, even to death; remain here, and stay awake with me." -Matthew 26:38

Why do they want to kill me
What have I done
Is it normal to kill your son?

Jesus came to a place called Gethsemane. Laying down, the condemned looked around at the only home he'd really ever known. Though they heard Jesus, the disciples just couldn't pay attention. They knew the moment was serious. The problem was that all of their energy was gone. Whispering to the folks in the cells around him, the condemned said, "Sit here while I go over there and pray." To the folks in the two closest cells, the condemned begged for them to stay awake and pray with him. Jesus went a few steps further. Collapsing, the condemned shouted out, "Is there any other way?" When Jesus came back and everyone was sleeping, he said, "You pieces of shit couldn't stay awake for another hour?" Even though the condemned was furious, the hour was too close to be angry. The condemned asked again, "Can someone please stay awake with me?" Jesus didn't want to fall victim to the temptation of turning back in the face of death. Praying, the condemned asked, "Is this your will?" Jesus already knew the answer. The hour arrived. "I thought y'all were coming later. I'm still asleep." "Well, wake up!" The condemned saw the guards coming down the hallway. "But, I thought we were friends." No one is friends on the way to the execution. "Get up, let's go..." The van was silent. Jesus looked out the window. The condemned pondered the past.

"...I was in prison and you visited me." Jesus doesn't say, "I was not guilty in prison, and you came to me." Jesus binds his flesh with the flesh of those who have no hope. Willie Trottie is left with little hope. Tonight, the State of Texas will kill Trottie by lethal injection. We love to say it like that. If we can name the State of Texas as the perpetrator, we can follow in the footsteps of Pilate and wash our hands of the crime. Who are we really killing? Whose blood is to be shed tonight? Do we have the guts to answer such questions? If you believe the words of Matthew 25:36, the person to be strapped to the gurney is none other than Jesus.

The unfathomable love and grace of God is what binds Willie Trottie to the person of Jesus. The murders of Barbara and Titus Canada cannot keep Trottie from such grace and love. Why is this so difficult to believe? I think we want vengeance. We want blood. "Hate your enemies and kill those who persecute you." Can you imagine if our wants were actually the message of Jesus? I actually can. I see the message of hate played out each time we demand the blood of another. I don't see much Jesus in killing and all of us here seem love to kill. When will we stop? I want us all to get saved from killing.

I feel like Jesus is calling for us all to choose love, but we refuse to pick up. To assuage our consciences, we will pretend as if nothing is happening. We clutch our children and give no thought to the mother in Huntsville who just clutched the glass as she watched the life drain out of her child. We will kiss those we love and not consider those who just kissed someone they love goodbye. We will glance over the news with assurance that all will glance over the crime that we just committed. In all of these actions, we will forget that we were made for each other. When will we remember?

There will be much forgetting after tonight. People will go on about their lives as if nothing ever happened, and many will go to church. Pastors will offer communion in the coming days. The problem is that the communion our churches offer will not be real. For, it is impossible to have real communion when no one knows if they will be the next one killed. The God that is celebrated will be a fraud. For, how can anyone claim to believe in a God that kills because of anger and vengeance? For people who claim to follow Jesus here, we are the great pretenders.

We torture people. Jesus sweat blood in those final hours. The condemned experience the same agony. I thought we opposed torture. We don't. We love it. What do you call forcing someone to sit in a smell cell in agony waiting to be executed? People respond to torture by breaking down. I guess that's the point. A broken human doesn't appear to be a real human. Unreal humans are much easier to kill.

There is always a final appeal. People seem to enjoy having the power of life and death in their hands. Refusing to break, Jesus approached the authorities and declared, "I am exactly what I've always said that I am." The condemned shouted out, "Innocent!" No one listened. People don't want to listen. There is no reward in listening. If you listen too carefully, you don't get to kill. In the midst of the final appeal to the authorities, the condemned heard something outside. "Crucify that monster!" "Kill him!" "Murder the murderer!" People were shocked to see the blood thirst come to life. Jesus was not. For many years, Jesus prepared for this day. The voices were very familiar. The final appeal would not succeed. They rarely do. "Crucify him!" "Crucify him!" "Crucify him!" There was no turning back. Death was in the air.

Trottie is right here
Feel all the fear
Cut out the lights
It's execution night

I knew where he was. The frigid room was always the same: booths for visiting; chains clanking against the floor.; guards barking orders; vending machines dropping snacks; everyone on edge. People die in these facilities. You can't ignore death here. You have to encounter it and see it for what it is. There was death in the air on that day. Tim and I talked about the case. The crime was fairly run of the mill on death row. In the throes of passion, Willie Trottie killed his ex-wife and her brother. While my characterization might sound strange to folks on the outside, killings are characterized on death row. Honestly, if you're not a serial killer or a killer of children, most inmates wonder why you're even back there. These folks are supposed to be the worst of the worst. These folks are supposed to be monsters. Don't get me wrong, there are plenty of terrifying people back there. But I guess you learn to contrast when you visit regularly. Comparing killers is an interesting business. Crimes of passion look a little less terrifying. Regardless, I prayed for Trottie. I knew that only a miracle would save him now. Did Jesus pray for Jesus when the hour started to get close? Tim looked at me and said, "Why do followers of Jesus do this?" I could only pray. "Oh Jesus, turn our bodies into keepers of love instead of keepers of killing." As we finished our visit, I looked up. Trottie was still there. I knew where I needed to go. The frigid room was always the same. Room of life. Room of death. "The hour is here."

I knew the exact spot. I'd looked in the death booth before. I didn't know if anybody would get mad at me for stopping. I didn't want to find out. I only wanted to offer a bit of encouragement. Placing one foot in front of the other, I arrived at the space and stopped. Slowly, I turned around. Immediately, my eyes made contact with Trottie's. For a second, time was suspended. I could see the fear. How could there not be fear when one is waiting to die? Trottie seemed know who I was. Maybe he'd seen a picture of some of my abolition work or heard about my visits with his "friends." Regardless, I wanted to do something that would ease his mind. I was lost. I guess I thought so much about getting over to that spot, that I forgot to think about what to do when I arrived. There was no way Trottie was going to hear me. I knew that and so did he. There was something dumb about sitting there trying to mouth words to each other. What do you do when you're surrounded by death? What do you do when you can't stop it? What do you do when you feel like death is getting close enough to destroy you? Many of the people who watched Jesus carry the cross asked similar questions. I was there on the path to the execution. I was there demanding more from myself. I was afraid. I was standing on the sidelines. I couldn't do anything more than pray. Thoughts ravaged my brain in the seconds I looked at Trottie. Finally, I looked up and raised a lone fist of resistance. Trembling, Trottie raised a fist as well. We didn't need words. We embodied the resistance. I watched Trottie tremble his last. Strength seemed to burst forth like lightening. Trottie became the incarnation of Christ. As Trottie's fist unclinched, I knew that he was ready. A guard asked: "Everything okay?" I knew the question was meant to push me along. I walked. The metal slammed behind me: "Bam!!!" Even though I knew it was coming, I jumped. The noise shook my core. Trottie was about to die and there was nothing I could do about it. In fact, my citizenship made me one of his killers. I just kept walking… "Bam!!!" I wasn't prepared for that one either. I walked as fast as I could to the exit. One of the inmates looked up and asked, "Are you okay?" I knew I wasn't. I replied, "Someone is being executed today." "I'll pray." By the time I got to the car, I was a mess. Sweat collected. Tears were close. *What do I do? What do I do? What do I do?* Even though the world was on fire, I didn't have to think long. I knew that I had to follow the way God…the way of Willie.

Who was driving the car? What difference did it make? We knew the way. We were heading in the right direction. We turned right. We saw all sides of the facility. We turned right again. We saw the exit that the transport would shortly leave from. This was the way… the Via Dolorosa. Every bump was another voice. We could hear the people pushing him along. "Monster!" "I wish I could kill you myself." "You're getting out much easier than they did." We felt every bump. We leaned into every turn. "Maybe we shouldn't be killing people?" The turns gave us hope that this whole thing might turn around. "You filthy piece of trash." There weren't enough turns to matter. We kept pushing. The trees leaned over the roadway. We could hear them whispering their judgments. "You were a piece of shit from the moment you were born." "Every piece of your being is evil." God don't care about you." We turned right. The scent of the lakes made it feel like the pain was almost over. We were skeptical. "Save us." "It's a trap." "Where is God?" Right there, left at the church. "Burn in hell!" "God damn you!" "God hates murderers like you." The words cycled round and round. The grass whispered warnings. "Don't go any further." "Turn around!" "There is only evil up ahead." We kept going. Our job was to travel the way. Dirt mounds rose higher and higher. They were trying to get a better view. It's not every day that you get to see a murderer. The way grew longer. "Can't they hurry up?" "Why does there have to be a protocol?" "I wish they'd shoot him." We finally arrived at the hunting camp. We felt like we were being hunted. "Get him." "Pick him up." "Drag him." Right before we were about to be slaughtered, we drove over the most beautiful lakes imaginable. We dreamed of something else. No one kept count of the time. We slid in and out of reality. If there was ever a place to touch God on this journey, it was at the top of this bridge. "I never wanted my life to turn out like this." "I miss my family." "Forgive me." Tears flowed with the water. The wind carried us on. For a long time, we were pulled by the thoughts of what might have been. We kept passing churches. We knew there wasn't any salvation in those joints. God was with us. We thought we might need to stop for gas. Something else was pushing us. The way held us. The way moved us. The way drove us on. "I am with you always." Repeatedly knocked unconscious by the pain of it all, we didn't know how we got there. The town was ready. Nothing was going to stand in the way of the execution. We drove up to Golgotha. There was a gate to enter. We dared not go. We knew death lived in those rooms. "This is where you will wait." "The procedure is painless." "In just a few shorts hours, the execution will be performed." We were stuck. We wanted to go in. We wanted to be there as they crucified our God. We were scared. Everyone else ran away. We got as close as we could. "Please God help me!" The cell grew smaller and smaller as the hour drew closer. What do you talk about when you know the conversation is going to be your *last? When your family comes? "I love you." When your lawyer comes in? "I love you." When your friends come in? "I love you." When the guards come in? "I love you." Love is often all that the mind knows in such circumstances. Where love is, God is. The anxiety grew. War raged in heaven. "Why can't we just finish this!" The terrified man was being pulled to the gurney. "We got a dead man walking!" "Are there any final appeals?" Medical professionals were acting against their professions to commit great evil. Everyone seemed to be acting against their professional oaths. He was strapped down. The straps looked extra tight. We figured that this must be what happens to an enemy of the state. The microphone came down and the final words caught some and no one by surprise, "Find it in your hearts to forgive me." We extended the words of grace. The statement extended the words of grace to us. Salvation flowed between us. The way brought us to this place of divinity. The poison flowed like a mighty river. He was drowning. Eyes closed. Breath stopped. Heart gone. "It is finished." We were in tears. This was routine to the employees. The government orders it. I saw a few people trying to wash their hands, but it doesn't wash off. When killing becomes routine, we are all beyond washing. We cried. What else is anyone to do when a killing happens? We couldn't just stand there. Eventually, we walked away. Multiple people cast lots for what was left. We thought the way was over. When we got back in the car, we realized who had been with us...God, Jesus, and the Spirit of the Executed. They'd never stopped speaking to us. "I am with you always." "I am with you always." "I am with you always."*

There is power
Oh, that's often unseen
You don't have to ask for it
Just learn to be

Though I didn't want to go back there, the Spirit led us to the cemetery behind the execution site. "Let the dead bury the dead." We were given sight. The Executed were constantly coming back and forth. Jesus was with us. We knew that the resurrection was amongst us. I looked up and saw the Executed taking people to the place beyond execution. There was no more evil. There was no more pain. There was only the redemptive power of love.

Excitement overcame us. We jumped. We cheered. Our entire bodies shook. "Come, Almighty God!" The world seemed to fade into a blur. My eyes shot open. I heard the final words. "Follow me."

Behold, I saw God lean up. "Killing is wrong." I couldn't tell who was speaking. "I repent."

CONCLUSIONS

Behold, I saw needle catch the vein. The poison started to flow. I trembled at the horror.

You can't follow Jesus without running to his execution. The gurney is the only place of salvation. Only cowards run away. Those who persevere to the end of all this shit will be saved.

The chronology of scriptures started to blur. There was no order. Time dissipated. Something was happening...

The Road to Austin

"...scales fell from [Saul's] eyes..." -Acts 9:18

Blistered feet
Heavy hearts
Broken tears
God got lost

The Spirit took me back. For a few years, I lived the life of a serial killer. While I didn't physically kill anyone, I felt like I wasn't doing enough when the government killed in my name. Did I speak out? No question. Did I make posts on social media? Absolutely. Did I go to events? For sure. Did I sign petitions? I did all of this and more. It wasn't enough. We're not called to give all that we *can*. We are called to give all that we *are*. I was going through the motions. We all do. Our spiritualities go no deeper than simply needing to feel good about ourselves. How can anyone feel good in the midst of the heinous atrocity that is the death penalty? How can anyone feel good about being made a serial killer by their government? There is no good. There is only God. Our call is to always go much deeper than good. Our call is to give our body to solve what we created.

Names are funny things. When your life changes, sometimes you need a name that fits the circumstances. Saul eventually became Paul. Before he did, he did some nasty shit. Fearful of the growth of another spirituality, Saul went around killing people. Stoning was his favorite method of execution. The blood flowed.. If anyone dared question him, Saul would simply assert his religious beliefs. How many times have we heard that shit before? Many atrocities have flown out of deep religious conviction. I know some "Sauls." I bet you do too. I think it was all of those "Sauls" who got us into this mess. They take religion and make it something horrible. That's how we got to the death penalty.

I'll never forget. Wind swirled. Stars sat high in the sky. While I had on a big coat, it wasn't big enough. Light flooded the front of the prison. If I hadn't been there many times before, it would've been easy to confuse the clock and the moon that night. Regardless, I wasn't looking at the clock. I was looking *behind* it. The darkness seemed to reveal something. There in the distance was the outline of a cross. Though I'd seen the cross before, I'd never seen it like this. The harder I looked, the more truth was revealed. I believe I went into some kind of trance. The cross drew closer and closer. I felt like I couldn't take it. I felt like the cross was going to overcome me. Though I've always wanted to be close to the cross, this was too much. "You did this." The cross, raised high above the execution chamber, spoke to me. "Christians created your death penalty." Looking up, I declared, "God, tell me it isn't so…" "It is so." The vision flooded my brain. I watched the bloody sacrifices of animals flow to the bloody sacrifice of Jesus, then flow to theologies centered on bloody sacrifices that flow into our bloody practices of vengeance. We are all about the blood. Unfortunately, the blood might be the biggest problem. If you are taught that blood is required for sin, executions are going to make sense to you. The gurney is our modern altar. We don't worship God. We worship the perceived elimination of sin. We are total dumbasses. Violence creates more violence. The more people we kill, the more killers we will create. You don't teach people not to kill by killing. You teach people not to kill by *not killing*. Our theology is so fucked up. So is our practice. The cross overlooking the execution chamber haunted my soul. I had to do something. My body was all that I had to give. I don't know when Saul actually became Paul. I only know that he changed somewhere along the way.

Community leaders of the day stood with their stones ready. The law said that the woman caught in adultery was to be killed. Everyone looked up to see what Jesus would do. Joining the woman in the dirt, Jesus used his body to save her. Without the body of Jesus, the woman would have perished.

I seek to emulate Jesus. Community leaders of our day here in Texas and around the country stand with their stones ready for another execution. Here is my response.

Over the next few days, I will give my body to the struggle to abolish the death penalty. I will pilgrimage 200 miles from Livingston to Austin to help my neighbors understand that you cannot love your neighbor as your self, and execute them. With every step I take, I will pray for an end to the violent crimes committed by both individuals and through state-sponsored executions. I know the God who was a victim of a violent execution is with me.

I am seeking to love my neighbors as I never have before and I pray that the world will follow suit.

I thought I had it together. Then, I realized I didn't. We hadn't even left yet and my entire body gave out. I didn't have anything to hold on to. I just landed on the floor. Now, I'm not one for quiet times. I don't think planned prayer with God is all that beneficial.

I think God is more of an experience than a prayer. If we are who we are, then we reflect the image of the God who created us. Our job is to hold onto the reflection. When I found myself on the floor, I started singing an old song: "I want God to walk with me. I want God to walk with me. All along life's pilgrim's journey, I want God to walk with me." Those words were my constant prayer. I knew that I was a follower of Jesus walking into a world of Sauls. Was it my time? I knew that at any moment one of those Sauls could get me. Would it happen at the prison? Would it happen along the road? Would it happen at one of my events? Would it happen? I didn't know. I just knew what I had to do.

Roads comfort me. I often find myself on bright days and dark nights between strips of white and yellow paint. When I meet him, I often wonder who he is and what he has done with my self. The confusion lets me know that I am still alive and perhaps growing in my humanity. There is something comforting about being reminded that we are still alive. This is a story about roads and life.

My heart was full. My heart is always full when I travel to Livingston. From rainy drives to sunny drives, I always feel the same on the way down…full. I had my first visit of the trip when I pulled into town. There were tears and love in that place. Regardless of the crime, I knew I had just encountered a child of God. I didn't want to leave. I never want to leave. It always hurts to feel like you are leaving someone in such desperate need of love.

I pulled up to the hotel and took a few pieces of clothing out of the car. I nearly forgot my medicine, but I knew that my physiology couldn't handle the fullness of the next few days without the right amount of medicine in my system. I got up to the room and started to pray. "God, make me an instrument of your peace…and if I die…let it be for you." I was scared. I had never walked this far in my life and there were so many unknown variables. Prayerfully, I pressed on to morning.

The door slammed behind me. The Polunsky Unit is good at making everyone who enters feel like a monster. I sat down across from a man I'd been visiting for some time. We chatted about love and courage. I never grow tired of these topics…especially in a place so devoid of hope.

I told him that I was about to do a 200-mile pilgrimage, and he told me to walk for him…and I did.

The door slammed behind me. I jumped out of the car in my robe and stole to begin my walk. I said a brief prayer and turned the corner to start walking away from the Polunsky Unit. I made it five minutes before one of the guards from the residence of the warden drove up in a van and rolled down the window with his hand on a shotgun. "What are you doing out here?" "Walking." "Where are you going?" "To Austin." "That's a long walk. Why are you walking?" "I love Jesus and oppose the death penalty." "Well, you need to hurry up and get out of here." I walked faster.

There was a beautiful shade tree that invited me to stop next to the road. It was hot and I paused to briefly collect myself. There was sweat dripping off both my glasses and face. There was a truck that slung into the driveway next to the tree and an angry young man jumped out to scream at me. "This is private property!" "Where does the right of way begin and I will move." "Right there where that ditch is and if I see you so much as take a step over that line…you will regret it." I held the line.

The gas stations and restaurants were unique experiences. Everyone stared and many commented. "What in the fuck are you wearing?" "Are you gay?" "That is an amazing costume." A blue minivan swerved to the side of the road. "Do you need a ride?" "No, I am on a pilgrimage to abolish the death penalty." "I am for the death penalty. Why are you against it?" "Because I am a Christian." "I am a Christian too, and I am still for the death penalty. Why do you think being a Christian has anything to do with opposing the death penalty?" "Because I don't believe you can love your neighbor as your self and execute them." "Damn, that makes sense. I'm going to have to think about that some more." She said goodbye and drove away.

The sun was going down as I crossed the bridge over Lake Livingston and the Trinity River. I wept at the beauty of the moment, or I wept out of exhaustion… I am still not sure which. I journeyed over to the side of the road to prepare a place to go to sleep. As I nodded off, I couldn't believe that this was only just the first day and I prayed that God would somehow give me the strength to finish.

I don't think I had that moment on the Road to Damascus. I do think there were many "moments" on the Road to Austin. When people yelled at me, I knew that I was meeting Sauls along the journey. Truthfully, I guess we don't know the difference sometimes between the Sauls and Pauls. They look the same. Sometimes, they might even act the same. I didn't spend much time trying to figure out who was who. I just assumed that God was transforming everybody into abolitionists. There was too much road to cover to get bogged down in nuance. I had more body to give. I prayed then as I pray now, for the abolition of the death penalty.

Sleeping isn't easy when you're not on a bed. We take our rest for granted. Homelessness is a pervasive problem in our world. We do violence everyday when we don't consider the sleepless nights of others. I spent the first few waking hours of my second day on pilgrimage walking against the death penalty and thinking about homelessness.

To say that it was hot on my pilgrimage is like saying that Antarctica is cold. My body consistently produced more sweat than I could've ever imagined possible. The robe I was wearing felt like being wrapped in a wet sheet. Regardless, I kept on walking to my next stop… the home of the Texas Execution Chamber.

Huntsville is a typical small town. Most people work for the local company…the Texas Department of Criminal Justice. Wesley Memorial United Methodist Church is a bastion of hope in a space often darkened by a refusal of the people to engage in serious conversation around topics of social justice.

I walked into the church and the people greeted me with open arms. I spent the first 20 minutes telling my story, and then I heard from the gathered their stories. We came to a conclusion that Jesus loves us all more than we will ever know and that is the most important thing to carry with us. It was a beautiful evening. When I thought I couldn't be moved further by their hospitality, a woman appeared with a basin full of water to wash my feet. Jesus lives in Huntsville. I met her.

Upon pilgrimaging to the Huntsville Unit (the site of the Texas Execution Chamber), I placed my hands on the brick wall. "May the cross that is on top of this place...be the cross that leads the State of Texas to stop perpetuating the cycle of violence by killing people. Make me an instrument of such peace." I departed into the cold dark night.

The porch of the abandoned trailer was very lonely. I didn't know if I was going to be safe or not. My phone died and I didn't know if the folks I was counting on knew where I was. When the car pulled up, I was gushing. I would sleep in a bed tonight and arise to walk another day.

I had worried about violence and anger when I walked into Huntsville. As I laid my head down on a soft pillow, I worried about violence and anger as I thought about walking into Brazos County the next day. I prayed for God to keep me from fear. God didn't...but I decided to walk anyway.

When our hearts change, we expect to be alone. I wasn't. A beautiful crowd greeted me. In the heat, I thought it must be a mirage. It wasn't. There was a group of people standing there cheering my every step. Seconds earlier, I'd been so tired. Now, I felt like I could run the rest of the way. God gives us strength at the most unexpected times. It was almost as if I could reach out and touch God. Truthfully, God reached out and touched me. In the corner, a woman pulled out a basin. I'll never forget the sound of water splashing around my feet. I knew that God was touching me. I was blinded by it all.

I was not too far over the Brazos County line when a Sheriff's Deputy rolled up. Jumping out of the car, the Deputy started a line of call and response with me, "Where are you going?" "To Austin" "Walking?" "Yes, I am walking from Livingston to Austin in protest of the death penalty." "Okay..." Then another officer pulled up and jumped out of the car. "Can we take a look at your license? We just want to make sure that dispatch has your name and knows that you are going to be walking." "Sure." The officer proceeded to check for prior arrests and warrants. I was thoroughly investigated for walking down the road. The entire situation made me think about the numerous persons who are put through a similar situation without the benefit of being able to speak English...often for the same reason that I was...walking.

I got my sweat on after the incident, until I was stopped by a photographer/videographer for the local newspaper to do some interviews and pose for some pictures. When you can barely walk, you feel weird participating in such rituals...but you do it in order to get the message out. I kept on moving after the media interaction was over. I felt like I walked all day needing to take a shit. There are very few bathrooms on the way into Bryan or College Station. Then I saw it...the closest thing to paradise I'd seen in some time...a hole-in-the-wall honky tonk called "The Beer Joint."

Pushing the doors open with force, I walked in and spoke past the five guys sitting on bar stools to the woman working behind the counter. "Can I please use your restroom?" "Of course." Before I could get to the restroom though, a man at the bar turned to ask, "What in the hell are you doing?" I guess they had never had someone come in with clergy vestments on before. "I am walking from Livingston to Austin in protest of the death penalty." "Why in the hell would you do that?" "Because I am a Christian." "That sounds pretty silly to me." "I promise I'll come back out and tell you why it is not silly after I get done using the bathroom." "Go right ahead. I ain't trying to hold you up." I took one of the most impactful and freeing shits of my life before I came back out to have a long conversation about the death penalty and faith with the guys at the bar and the woman working behind the counter. Before I left, most of the folks present told me they admired what I was doing whether they agreed with me or not. I left and started walking once more.

Sweating profusely and in a good deal of pain, I made it until about four miles from the Brazos County Courthouse. I called the reporter who was to interview me that evening over dinner, and asked her to come pick me up. I was exhausted. The reporter drove me by the Brazos County Courthouse, where I prayed for District Attorney Jarvis Parsons to stop pursuing death sentences. I asked that Jesus would manifest in the life of this deeply religious man in a way that would not let him participate in the killing of anyone else. I got back in the car. Upon arriving at the Mexican restaurant, I waxed poetic the rest of the night with the reporter about life, faith, and the death penalty.

When I laid my head down, I was comforted to know that the next day I would not be walking alone.

So often, we walk blindly through life. We see the presence of God and can't equate it with reality. People keep killing each other. Yet, we have been told that there is a higher way. I was trying to get through. It is hard to keep walking when the end seems so far away. It is hard to move when violence is raging all around you. I just kept walking. When I encountered law enforcement, I couldn't see why they were so worried about me. I was more worried about them.

I woke up. I woke up. I woke up. The transition from sleep to engagement with the world was difficult. I felt terrible. This was only to be my fourth day on my pilgrimage. How would I survive? I prayed and started to force my bones to move.

Still moving slowly, I met a group of people who would walk down the middle of College Station and Bryan with me. We talked about the death penalty. The weather transformed the conversation quickly. There were not many steps before we transitioned to talking about how miserably hot we were. When we got to the church, I had soaked through my robe again. Traveling in a hot wet robe yhat transforms into a cold, wet, inside robe causes you feel like you are turning into a sea lion.

I climbed into the pulpit. I was so nervous. This was the first time I'd ever preached in a Roman Catholic Church before. I thundered down about needing to place our bodies into the conversations concerning social injustice. I had spoken about such things previously, but now I was truly starting to embody and believe it in a new way. After about 15 minutes, I said, "Amen." There were awkward moments between the time of reflection and the time of departure. I didn't know who was supposed to dismiss the group. The "awkward" blossomed to "beautiful" when I stood up and the people came to the aisles to bless me on the way out. The love of God flowed through the many hands that were placed on my body as I walked by. I now had the strength to finish.

Walking through the dirt and grass, I yearned for what I knew was approaching. The sun hit my eyes in a majestic reflection of light when

I stumbled forward. I stooped down to drop both my hand and soul into the Brazos River. All of my sins were redeemed. I felt cleansed. I knew that I had to continue… I had to continue sounding the alarm of what the death penalty is doing to our souls.

Night was rapidly approaching as I stumbled through Caldwell looking for something to eat. I found a Chinese restaurant still open. I gobbled up strawberries, fried rice, and coconut shrimp, and washed it all down with a cold Sprite. CNN was running a show about the anniversary of O.J. Simpson and the white Bronco. For some reason, I felt like the struggle to abolish the death penalty was similar to the situation playing out before my eyes on television again… It is a tragedy from start to finish.

I got bed bugs overnight.

The awakening often leads to a greater blindness in our world. Make no mistake, the rest of our society is blind. The death penalty is symptomatic of our inability to see our own spiritual paralysis. Throughout the walk, I kept reminding myself that most people in our society simply can't move. I was walking alone because of the paralysis that has afflicted the consciousness of our society. We think we can kill our way to something better. We can't. We need new brains. The ones we have are simply not working. We need an experience with God. That's the only thing I know that can make the scales fall off. Rain came. I think it started to loosen the scales.

Storms were coming that looked fierce but never truly developed into anything but a short shower.
Red bumps covered the skin of my right hip. Each step I took caused my robe to rub up against those bumps and made them itch more. I knew I was in for a hot, itchy day.

The wet, hot, dusty asphalt and rocks of Highway 21 were the most miserable part of my entire journey. I had trouble balancing, and stumbled around. I prayed for help at numerous junctures. On more than one occasion, I had to decide to force my back to straighten a bit and simply keep walking.

One of the major stories to come out about my walk went to press in the middle of the day... I was highly encouraged. I knew that the article would shed much light on the death penalty in Texas. I walked faster...I guess, because I felt like we were making progress.

After almost more two full days of walking, I made it all the way to Bastrop. I conquered physical infirmity and boredom to begin my final two days of descent into Austin.

The bed bugs kept me company.

Amidst the rain, I stopped for a rest under a bridge. I pushed through all sorts of feelings of guilt about stopping. I told myself it would just be for a minute. It wasn't. I was blind to my own tiredness. The robe grew heavier with every step. I think the weight of the death penalty made it so. After a few prayers, I leaned back. I was gone. The dreams were all over the place. When I woke up, darkness found me. I looked over and there was a big pile of shit. I didn't know what the shit was supposed to represent. I just knew that it smelled like shit. I woke up as quickly as I gone to sleep. Once I got back to the road surface, I started walking. The scales came off. I could see. Everything was clearer. Coming out of the sky, I could see God taking every step. Turning around, I could see countless people walking with me. Where were all of these people coming from? I didn't know. I just knew where we were going. We were abolishing the death penalty. Spirituality begins with a step.

I got saved that night
Deep in a big smelly pit
I got saved that night
Running away from that shit

"Do you remember?" I can't forget. My feet were on fire. The roads changed from rural to urban. I felt like I was going to be hit by a car at any moment. I didn't have time to pray. "Get out of the way, you idiot!" Every step would have to do.

Walking down a busy highway late in the day was different than anything I'd done before. People were honking and yelling as I walked. I don't think anyone was honking and yelling because they liked the look of a man in a robe either. I was unnerved. I thought about stopping. I was tired. I wondered what it would be like to stop. I kept going.

The sidewalks disappeared and I trudged through the tall grass. I felt like I had bugs in every crevice of my body. I walked.

I arrived at a motel on the outskirts of Austin. Sleep came quickly. I knew that I was almost done.

God is drawing us home. I feel it. By the time I got to that hotel, I knew I could make it.

There is nothing like waking up and knowing that you're going to finish. I knew that every step was a step toward abolishing the death penalty. I called and talked to many people throughout the day as I walked into Austin. I stopped for some lemonade. The sweetness of the taste almost made me forget the pain in my feet and legs. I pushed on with lemonade in hand.

Two fellow pilgrims greeted me on South Congress Avenue and walked with me the rest of the way, holding signs opposing the death penalty. Their presence was comforting. Multiple blocks later, two of my dear friends met me along the way. One of my friends had on a "LGBT Pride" shirt. I didn't think anything of it...until someone drove by screaming out of a truck window "Fuck you, faggot!" There is nothing like a little phobia and hate to try and ruin a moment of triumph. We didn't let it... We just kept on walking.

Excitement filled all of us as we crossed the street and planted our feet on the grounds of the Capitol of Texas. I felt electricity shooting out my toes. The gathered friends and supporters began to clap and cheer as we walked up. I gave a brief statement and we walked into the Capitol. I stopped for a brief second to pray in the rotunda before moving on toward our closing event at University Baptist Church.

During the program, I talked over and over about the need to give our bodies to the struggle for justice. After my walk, I believe the group *understood what I meant. I can think of no more fitting a place to finish my journey than where it began...in a Baptist church.*

I walked for life. I walked for love. I walked for us.

"Did you think you were going to finish?" "No. No, I didn't. Look at my feet! I got so depressed. Look at my brain! I got beat up by the conditions. Look at my soul! I'm so weary." "How can I possibly look at those things?" "Come and take a walk with me."

Waiting

"...he ordered them not to leave..." -Acts 1:4

Oh, Robert Ladd
He, really ain't that bad

People stood outside the prison. Where else could they go? The walls held something you couldn't get anywhere else. God whispered in the trees. The wind seemed to carry the voice of the condemned. Everybody stands out there waiting for a sign. It's the same spot every time. Can you imagine waiting for someone to be executed? While people say all sorts of things, the reality quickly becomes apparent that there is nothing to do but pray. The harder you push your requests to heaven, the more you hear from those who have already gone before. If you will turn your attention to the heavens, there are lessons to be learned. Their final words always seem to linger. In the midst of an outbreak of executions, I pondered whether or not prayers are heard in that place. I've waited for the state to kill too many times. How could God be out there? Late that night, I started to pray...

God, Why? Why do I have to keep coming down here? Why was Robert Ladd born with mental disabilities? Why were people murdered? Why are we about to murder Robert Ladd? Why? Do you care? Are you here? Is there a reason why you don't stop this? Are you addicted to death and suffering? Do you even exist? I don't know the answer to these questions. I only know that I have chosen to believe. I believe that you are there with Robert. I believe that you will walk with Robert down the hallway. I know that you will lay down with Robert on the gurney. I know you will feel the needle. I know that you will die with Robert. You have taught me to believe that death doesn't happen without resurrection. I know that you will not leave us here as murderers. I know that you will resurrect us to meet Robert and ask for his forgiveness for our sins.

"I'm very, very sorry." I knew that Ladd had asked for forgiveness. I could feel it in my bones. Why didn't anyone in the room ask Ladd for forgiveness? This was an execution, wasn't it? An mentally disabled convicted killer had more decency than the entire government that executed him. I watched all of those officials walk out. I wondered what was festering in their hearts. How could words of forgiveness not fester? They were. God ordered them not to leave. God told them to wait on something new. Whether they use them or not, God has given them new words. I think they will rumble around until they can't contain them anymore. Surely, all those folks will get saved from killing. Surely, all those folks will learn to ask for grace as Ladd had. We didn't move. It was almost as if God had ordered us not to leave. When the Spirit came upon us, I looked up the heavens. There is something about all those stars out there. Each burst of light seems to add drama to it all. That night, I could hear the great choir of witnesses in millions of tongues shouting out, "Grace! Grace! Grace!" I wanted to be with them. Robert Ladd was there. I believe I spoke a new tongue when I started chanting in unison, "Grace! Grace! Grace!" I didn't move. The chill of the night welcomed me home.

The Spirit Failed

"When the day of Pentecost had come..." -Acts 2:1

Names of people
Rejected by your steeple
They all died
Longing to be inside

Recognize any of these names? Linwood Briley. Ernest Knighton. Morris Mason. Carroll Cole. Connie Ray Evans. Leo Edwards. Connie Dunkins. Buddy Earl Justus. Hoyt Clines. Harold Otey. Mario Marquez. Hai Hai Vuong. Earl Matthews. D.H. Fleenor. Wanda Jean Allen. Marilyn Plantz. Sahib Al-Mosawi. James Willie Brown. Holly Wood. Teresa Lewis. Elmer Carroll. Jerry Correll. Travis Hittson. They are the condemned. They are the forgotten. They are the executed. This list contains the random names of 23 of the more than 1437 who have been executed in the United States since 1976. I hadn't heard of many of them before compiling their names. Why do some of the condemned become known and some remain unknown? I don't know the answer to that question. I guess it has something to do with the confusion of it all.

Everyone was in the same place. Suddenly, there was a rush of a mighty wind. Then, tongues of fire fell down from heaven. Disciples joined together to push back against death. "Not one more!" There was no response. Rage took over. "No more executions!" "No more executions!" "No more executions!" The cry grew louder and louder. People started pushing against the lines. Assorted tongues took over. There were people demanding an end to the madness in every possible language. Over and over, the people pumped their fists and rocked back and forth. Nobody wanted to wait another second for the killing to stop. "Abolish the Death Penalty Now!" The crowd seemed to grow. I knew some people there.. "Abolition!" Everyone wanted the same thing. There was unity in the extreme diversity of the moment. Though there were all sorts of tongues, everyone could understand each other. No one was left out. Every name was important. Together, the group kept lifting up names. "Gary Gilmore." "Charlie Brooks." "Karla Faye Tucker." "Kimberly McCarthy." "Lisa Coleman." "Robert Neville, Jr." In the whirlwind, it became apparent that the Spirit rests on those who are willing to say all the names. In the midst of it all, everybody heard every name. We knew that this wouldn't be the last time. I guess we were confused in order to go and do the confusing.

Kelly Gissendaner. I don't remember the first time I heard the name. It's quite possible that I was a teenager watching the news. The case was quite famous in our area. In any case, I knew that

I'd heard it before. There are some names that stick harder than others. Over the years, I'd kept up with a variety of cases. I wasn't watching the case of Gissendaner. It wasn't that I didn't care. I just couldn't follow them all. There were too many of them. Late one afternoon, I got a call from home. "You need to check out this case." I can tell when the Spirit starts to lead. Before long, I was immersed. Multiple friends were directly engaged in the struggle. The case exploded. People all over the country wanted to save Gissendaner. People from all types of backgrounds started to speak in new tongues. Pentecost was upon us. I wrote to do what I could do to try and save Gissendaner's life. The execution was quickly approaching. In the midst of death, I pushed back. Using a new language, I stood and delivered. We needed more bodies:

In February of 1997, Kelly Gissendaner orchestrated the brutal murder of her husband Doug in Gwinnett County, Georgia. Sentenced to die in 1998, Gissendaner's appeals process is about to run out. Barring a miracle, Gissendaner will be executed by the State of Georgia on Wednesday night (2/25/2015). Those of us who grew up in the South know well how this process of execution plays out. Over and over again, we watch society dispose of what we perceive to be our most brutal killers. Unfortunately, we fail to realize that no one has a right to kill anyone.

One day at the temple, Jesus met a woman similar to Kelly Gissendaner. The woman was tossed at his feet. The religious and government officials outlined her crimes and started to raise their instruments of execution. Instead of spending a bunch of time trying to convince or persuade the gathered government and religious figures, Jesus got down in the dirt with the woman. Now, if the religious and government officials were going to kill the woman, they were going to have to kill Jesus too. With great boldness, Jesus wrote the crimes of the religious and government officials in the dirt. In the midst of the confrontation, Jesus declared, "Let anyone among you who is without sin be the first to throw a stone...." The religious and government officials realized they weren't without sin and walked away. We all are just as guilty as Kelly Gissendaner, and no one has the right to take her life.

Most people think that the turning point of the story comes when Jesus writes in the dirt, or maybe when he speaks to the religious and government officials. I disagree with such assertions. The life of the woman was saved when Jesus placed his body in the dirt and was prepared to face the same punishment she was sentenced to. If we are willing to place our bodies into the conversation, Jesus shows us that we can save lives. Over the next two days, I pray that enough bodies will be placed into the conversation to save the life of Kelly Gissendaner. Bodies matter, and enough of them could abolish the death penalty once and for all. May God make it so.

We could all understand the new languages. I kept trying to get more people to listen. *Why were they still trying to execute her? Why were we still trying to execute her?* Things were so certain. We needed more confusion. We got it.

Twice the execution was stopped. How in the hell was that shit even possible? I had no faith. I absolutely believed that they were going to execute her during one of those attempts. I couldn't believe it. The first converts couldn't either. Using different languages, the converts converged to create the timidity that saved Gissendaner. They didn't kill her. They didn't kill her yet. Though, they were still ready to kill everyone else.

Kelly Gissendaner almost died for the sins of Christians. When word came in that Kelly's execution was postponed, I knew why she was almost executed beyond a shadow of a doubt. Having grown up in Georgia and now living in Texas, one grows familiar with these execution processes. Though there was much publicity around Kelly's case, most people are executed with little public resistance and scant media attention. If you look back a week to the night before Kelly was originally supposed to be executed, there was little attention being paid to the case. Then something spiritual happened. Christians in Georgia started to wake up.

The orchestrated effort to save Kelly's life was incredibly impressive. Post after post tagged #kellyonmymind filled social media. Popular Christian writers and bloggers offered their words of encouragement and resistance. The traditional media was full of stories about the changes that occurred in Kelly's life over the last few years. Professors, students, former inmates, and others created films that were incredibly compelling. The pictures that came out of the efforts of the last few days were unbelievable. Yet with all of this effort and attention, Kelly was saved by cloudy drugs, not public pressure. Now, we are left to wonder how we ever let her get so close?

When I say that Kelly almost died for the sins of Christians, I am being quite literal. The last death penalty case to get this type of attention was Troy Davis. I stood across the street from the prison in Jackson and watched the hundreds of people demand that the State of Georgia spare his life. I remember thinking that if we could keep up this moment, then we could abolish the death penalty all over the country. There have been five executions since the execution of Troy Davis. Most people could not name one name of the executed, let alone two. If Christians had been as excited and energized about stopping these last five executions as they were about stopping Kelly's, I don't think there would have been a death penalty to even talk about in this case. The lack of engagement from Christians around the country is what causes the heinous practice of executions to continue. Kelly almost died for the sins of Christians or the lack of engagement in the previous cases and efforts that could have saved the lives of everyone on death row. Will we now rest until they try to go through with the execution of Kelly again, or will we stand with the hundreds and hundreds and hundreds of people on death rows all over the nation facing execution?

After some of these cases garner tremendous public attention, I go back to my work as an abolitionist. I always pray that everyone will stay engaged and we can together abolish the death penalty. With seven executions scheduled here in Texas before the end of May, the lives of Kelly Gissendaner and Brian Terrell are still on the line, and numerous executions are scheduled across the country in coming days, abolitionists could sure use the help. #kellyonmymind must become #deathrowonmymind if we are going to end this heinous practice once and for all. Though I want to have hope, I always have to be realistic and tell myself that most of these Christians will probably just go back to doing what they were doing and not care about the wider sickness that is the death penalty. I pray that I am wrong.

The struggle was raw. I watched it unfold. In the midst of tons of people facing execution, the public seemed to only be concerned with one name, Kelly Gissendaner. Did people not understand that there were all sorts of other names of people trying to stay alive on death row? I was so angry that this sort of energy wasn't utilized earlier to abolish the death penalty for everyone. Where was all of this energy when my friend Juan Garcia was killed? I didn't want Gissendaner to die. I wanted everyone on death row to live. Pentecost turned into a nightmare. Everyone started using different languages. Things got more and more confusing. Now, the only thing certain was death. I raised my voice once again:

1.75 million Southern Baptists forced her down the hallway. 619 thousand United Methodists strapped her to the gurney. 596 thousand Roman Catholics pushed the needle in. 566 thousand Evangelicals assured everyone that this was God's will. As the poison started going in, there were millions of Georgia Christians participating in the homicide. Within minutes, Kelly Gissendaner died and Christians were the ones who killed her.

Upwards of 85 percent of Georgians identify as Christians. When Gissendaner was prosecuted, Christians pushed for the death penalty. When Gissendaner was sentenced, a jury of Christians sentenced her to death. When Gissendaner sat in prison, it was Christians who imprisoned her. When Gissendaner's final appeals were denied, it was Christians who pushed her to the execution chamber. When Gissendaner was executed, it was Christians who did the deed. Make no mistake... Christians killed Kelly Gissendaner.

There are some who might contest my categorizations by pointing to the fact that Christians are the ones who've been most involved in trying to save Gissendaner's life. I would argue that some of these persons are the ones most responsible for her death. What if this type of energy had been put into Gissendaner's case a decade ago? What if this type of energy would've been put into abolishing the death penalty altogether? I believe Kelly Gissendaner would still be alive. Christians love trying to save someone at the very last minute. What would happen if Christians started getting involved in the beginning? Over the next three months, there are 18 people facing the death penalty around the nation. Will they be on our minds? I hope so.

Everything was clear. The wind was gone. People were done. All of the energy was dried up. There was no fight left to try to save Kelly Gissendaner. There was only a bunch of people who should have fought against the death penalty long before this moment came. While the body was still warm, people started running back to their comfortable lives. The battle against the death penalty was lost. Everyone forgot that the death penalty continues to find victims. Maybe they didn't forget. Maybe they didn't care in the first place. Perhaps the cases that are all about the hype are truly all about the hype. For Gissendaner's sake, I wish something more had come much sooner. I wish something had saved her life. Prayer is all that was left. We gathered around. The loss of energy was unmistakable. "What is happening?" Emptiness reigned. Everybody repeatedly called out to God. *Nothing.* Nothing is all we heard. Pentecost had failed. After a few moments, it hit me, "We already executed God."

Kelly Gissendaner
Couldn't get no relief from Atlanta
Amazing grace
That's your song
When abolition hits
We gonna sing it all night long

Searching for Assurance

"Faith is the assurance of things hoped for, the conviction of things not seen." -Hebrews 11:1

OHIO
Toe to Toe
Here We Go

It's one thing to walk alone. It's a completely different thing to walk with others. I was learning how to be different. Community creates difference. We are called to walk. God chooses who we walk with. Our job is to believe in the unseen forces that bring everyone together. Spirituality is about movement. Where do we sit in the movement of the movement? God, *I want to be in that abolition number.* During those few days, I was:

"*...tell the Gissendaner family that I am so sorry. That amazing man lost his life because of me...*" *Just after midnight on September 30, 2015, after her final words of apology, the State of Georgia began to execute Kelly Gissendaner for the murder of her husband Doug. After the process started, Gissendaner began to sing:*

"Amazing grace! How sweet the sound
that saved a wretch like me!
I once was lost, but now am found;
was blind, but now I see."

The confluences of Gissendaner's remorse scramble around my brain like ants running around their home.

Tomorrow morning, I will start walking 83 miles from the Ohio Execution Chamber in Lucasville to the Ohio State Capitol in Columbus. A few months back when abolitionists in Ohio asked me to help lead their Walk to Stop Executions, I couldn't say no. Placing one foot in front of the other is the only path to abolition. Jesus walks too.

When I pilgrimaged 200 miles across Texas in 2014, the executed haunted me. This week will be no different. I will hear Kelly Gissendaner. I will feel Troy Davis. I will touch Kimberly McCarthy. I will experience Willie Trottie. I will speak Dennis McGuire. I will know Cameron Todd Willingham. I will experience them all. Like a fierce wind they will rage around me, speaking the words of God, "Prophesy to our breath!"
    I will...

While I am walking, my friend and fellow Texan Juan Garcia is to be executed on October 6. I clutch his picture right now. We only met once. I will never forget our powerful conversation. For two hours, we talked about the enormity of the love of God. I know that we deny the love with every execution. We've got to get saved.

One day, we will stop our murderous rampage of vengeance...in

Texas…in Ohio…and everywhere else. Until we do, I'm going to keep on walking.

I learned about my path by studying the paths of others. On the walk to Columbus, moments transpired to point us in the right direction. God often uses dumbasses to help out the cause. God is funny like that.

Car after car sped by. I looked into the eyes of every face. The image of God looked back. I spent the day walking for the abolition of the death penalty in Ohio. Every once in a while, someone would slow their car down, honk the horn, and raise a middle finger as high as possible. Their mouths made sure their meaning was not lost: "Fuck You!" Slowly, I got discouraged. Then, I got a word. The middle finger was pointing up to God as a reminder to pray for their ignorant asses.

When I was asked to pray in the middle of our pilgrimage to Columbus, I sought words that would lead to movement. I found them.

Spirit of Love. Spirit of Light. Spirit of Justice. Fill us from the tips of our toes to the tops of our heads with the passion and commitment necessary to end the death penalty. May the powerful words of abolition never be far from our lips. When we exit through the great wooden doors of this church and march out into the streets, let our cry ever be… "Not one more!" "Not one more!" "Not one more!" "Not one more!" "Not one more!" "Not one more!" "Not one more!" "Not one more!" "Not one more!" "Not one more!" Let it be so. Let it be so. Let it be so. Hallelujah!

Movement is not simply about physical movement. Movement is about the spiritual movement of the mind. Movement takes us beyond what is. The mind helps us turn dreams into reality. The mind is not constrained. The mind is blurry. When I was asked to deliver a lecture about the death penalty and the mind, I naturally had to blur the lines. We will never abolish the death penalty with our current lines. We must have the courage to follow God and go where our society has never gone before…to a place beyond killing. Eliminating the death penalty throughout our society is a good place to start. Faith is the assurance of things unseen. Let us journey toward the end.

Queer theorists and theologians push against boundaries and borders until they are no more and the individual is liberated to exist in the perfect freedom that is being. Cosmologists study origins and the development of the universe. Tonight, I intend to push us into a queer cosmological experience. The spiritual experience of thinking about the last questions of those on death row teaches us about our origins and helps us to think about how we can move to a space beyond boundaries and borders.

Just a few short weeks back, I spent a few hours visiting Juan Garcia. Though we've only knew each other for a short time, I've loosely based my talk tonight on some of the questions that Juan asked in our final meeting.

"Are you prepared to stand by as they kill me?"

The enormity of our cause should never be lost. We are participating in a struggle to save lives. Often, we are the last line of defense. The question of effort is a spiritual question. Do you believe in life enough to do all that you can to save it? To cede the question of life to the forces of death is a spiritual disease that has afflicted us for far too long. We must get rescued from our malaise. We must learn to push against the borders and boundaries of our laws that allow for executions to continually execute our consciences. Will we allow the machinery of death to continue with no resistance?

"Do you believe in forgiveness?"

We can't expect to change the way that people think about the death penalty until we change the way that we think about ourselves. Some of the most hateful and unforgiving people I know are abolitionists. How are we going to encourage our society to show mercy to persons on death row when we refuse to show mercy? Did you begin in hate? Abolition begins pushing against the borders and boundaries within.

"Is there redemption?"

The death penalty is a moral cancer on our society primarily because it refuses to acknowledge the possibility of redemption. Redemption is a critical component of a morally and ethically healthy society. Redemption allows people to change and blows up our categories of good and evil. I believe redemption is the only way to guide people to love. Do you remember love?

"What will the end be like?"

In order to get where we want to go,...we have to know what direction we are going. The eschatological question of the end is critical. Do you remember when we didn't have a death penalty? Do we want to be a society where all life is valued? I believe the end is love and that our job is to work toward getting there. Do you believe that abolition is possible? You must first learn to believe before you can start heading that direction. The borders and boundaries of the mind are always the most difficult obstacle to abolition.

Imagine that you have engaged all of these questions with someone who is condemned to die and the guard knocks on the door to tell you, "It's time." The doors open and you take the final steps with the condemned. As tears roll down your face...you enter the execution chamber. Walking up to the condemned on the gurney, you look down to offer one last word and you are shocked by the face you see...
It is your child.

This is how seriously we must begin to think about our origins and abolition of the death penalty.

By the time we arrived, I was exhausted. The walk to Columbus was so much longer than I anticipated. Our spiritualities experience different journeys. We are all pushing toward an end to killing. We all want abolition. We are all made in the image of God. When we walk, we are illustrating what it looks like to move toward the mover of movement. We are moving to move our world. Movement is at the heart of the movement. There will be no abolition of the death penalty until we move. In those days, we moved. God is still calling us to move. This is a prayer of movement:

Almighty God…We know you by many names…but today we gather for a primary purpose of abolition…but first we must repent. We repent that we wake up most days and don't give a shit about the death penalty. We repent that we've often mounted little resistance to the machinery of death. We repent that we've consistently supplied all the funds necessary…by way of our taxes…to carry out these executions. Oh God…we repent.

We thank you for the sweet spirit in this place…but God you know that we don't need any more sweetness. We know that it will take anger to abolish the death penalty. We know that we have to get angrier about these executions. Oh God…we pray for anger. We pray for anger so mighty that it turns into a rage strong enough to help us topple the whole damn system. We need anger against injustice. We need anger against killing. We need anger against the devaluation of life. We need anger…for we know that only anger and rage can lead us to a place of love. We have to overturn the gurney and execution tables, Lord, before we can learn to love the executioners. Help us, Oh God!

Raise our dead bodies up. Lift our weary feet. Grant us passion and commitment. Push us further than we ever thought we could go. May our Walk to Stop Executions turn into the Sprint to Abolition…and let it happen yesterday.

The walk into Columbus was amazing. People were very excited to celebrate the "coming demise of the death penalty." Everyone waved whatever they could get their hands on. Cameras from across the area captured the events. People were singing. People were chanting. People were ready for something more than what was. However, as we were crossing a bridge, I took a mental hit. My mind remembered Jesus entering Jerusalem before his execution. Looking around, I wondered if these folks looked like those folks. Regardless, I realized that maybe we weren't as close to the end as I thought.

I saw your face
Never stop walking

I heard your words
Never stop walking
I felt your pain
Never stop walking
I became you
Never stop walking

Monsters

"We know that those who are born of God do not sin..." -1 John 5:18

Down here, everyone thinks they're born of God. No one sins. So, everyone gets to sit in judgment of everyone else. These ideas of self-righteousness extend to the death penalty too. Long before the accused are convicted, people turn them into monsters and call for their deaths. There is nothing more holy in this part of the world than killing the monster. Jesus never taught any of this bullshit. John equated being born of God with sinlessness. John is full of shit. We have all sinned and fallen short of God. Why do we presume that these folks are any more worthy of death than all of us? Maybe we're the real monsters. Regardless, I've learned to walk with monsters. You should too. Your spirituality depends on it.

This Wednesday, Raphael Holiday will be executed minutes after 6 p.m. at the Walls Unit in Huntsville, Texas. Unlike many of those I've encountered on death row, I believe that Holiday deserves to die.

In early 2000, Raphael was partnered with Tami Wilkerson. Together, they lived in a secluded log cabin in Madison County with their infant daughter Justice and Tami's young daughters, five-year-old Jasmine and seven-year-old Tierra. In March, Tami discovered that Raphael had sexually assaulted Tierra and filed charges against him. Raphael was forced to move out. Despite the protective order, Tami let Raphael occasionally see his daughter. In August, Raphael started to assault and terrorize Tami incessantly. When she cut off all communication, things got worse.

Late in the night of September 5, 2000, Tami saw a figure coming through the woods. By the time family arrived to help, Raphael was in the house. Tami's aunt Beverly Mitchell rushed the oldest girls to the car. Though her uncle Terry Keller had a gun, Raphael choked Tami and made him hand it over. Raphael was unsuccessful in his attempts to burn the car with the girls in it. In the midst of it all, Tami rushed to a neighbor's home for help. Raphael forced all of the children back into the house. By the time Tami returned , the house was ablaze. Raphael burned young Justice, Jasmine and Tierra to death.

Though Raphael Holiday tried to argue that he didn't mean to kill the three little girls, I don't believe him. The jury didn't either. Now, the hour has come for the punishment to be carried out. I still believe that he deserves to die. There is only one question left to ask. Who deserves to kill him? I've sat with this question for many hours. I believe I know the answer.

There once was an execution scheduled. The authorities threw a woman that committed a capital offense at the feet of Jesus. As they raised their stones to kill her, Jesus got down in the dirt to join her in her fate. Looking up, Jesus declared, "Whoever is without sin can cast the first stone!"

Over the next two days, I will pilgrimage over 40 miles carrying the cross between Death Row/Polunsky Unit (noon on 11/17) in Livingston and the Execution Chamber/Walls Unit in Huntsville (6p.m. on 11/18) not because I believe that Raphael Holiday is innocent...but rather because I know he's not. Jesus taught us to "love our neighbors as ourselves," and Holiday has already shown us that there is no love in killing. May we show Holiday the mercy that he didn't show his victims. Throughout my journey, I will pray that we will stop emulating the killers we claim we are punishing and stop this foolishness of executions once and for all.

It was cold and wet. Regardless, I kept walking. Several miles from the execution chamber, I received word that a local judge had stopped Raphael Holiday's execution. I just knew that God had shaken the chains loose. I decided to keep going. I held my cross high in victory. Later, I was told that the local judge's order was reversed on appeal. Holiday would be executed that night. By the time I arrived at the chamber, jubilation had turned to mourning. This was a heinous crime. I pilgrimaged from Livingston with the full knowledge of who I was pilgrimaging for. I walked for someone everyone else calls a monster. I wish Christians would learn to truly be born of God and love their neighbor...even their "monster" neighbors. Through it all, I kept clinging to the cross. Amongst Holiday's final words before his execution were, "I love y'all." I wish we would've looked at Holiday and said the same thing. We didn't. We just killed him.

3 little girls
Wait, there's one more
Now, the body count is up to four

Community

"...since we are surrounded by so great a cloud of witnesses..."
-Hebrews 12:1

Morning came early. Church was a long way from home. In the midst of the moment, I thought about all the congregations that had come before. Everyone wants to talk about the abolition of the death penalty. No one wants to do it. It costs too much. I reflected on the cost of it all. I'd given all that I could muster. It didn't feel like enough. The God who could create anything didn't create a way out of all of this killing nonsense. Maybe, though, there is a way. We've always been told that Jesus is the way. That's why I brought my cross. I was still clinging to the idea that the cross illustrates the price of killing. I don't know that anyone else was thinking about it like that. Everyone just likes Jesus. Has anyone remembered the path of Jesus? Giving the body to save the bodies of others?

Step by step
Standing next to you
Laying our bodies down
There is work to do

District attorneys don't work on Sundays. There was nobody there to voice our complaints to. Heat overtook us before we took one step. I didn't pay it any mind. Pilgrimages are more about the heart than the mind anyway. We gathered around the cross. With one hand extended high and the other on the cross, I blessed the feet of those who carried the good news of abolition. For many miles, we walked for the killing to stop. We sang. We moved. We clapped. "How are we going to abolish the death penalty?" "We're *doing*." The community grew. There was a great cloud of witnesses. By the time we got to the church, we knew that we were going to abolish the whole damn thing with our voices alone. Though I preached for a considerable length of time, everyone was stuck on the names of the executed. I read them all. The great cloud of witnesses was bigger than anyone anticipated. When I looked out into the congregation, I could see that they'd all joined us.

Sacrament

"He was put to death in the flesh, but made alive in the spirit."
-1 Peter 3:18

Blood please
More blood please

We are a bloodthirsty people. We can't even get through Holy Week. Instead of remembering the execution of Jesus, we're preparing to execute Adam Ward. In 2005, Ward murdered City of Commerce Code Enforcement Officer Michael "Pee Wee" Walker. In 2016, we are preparing to do the same to him.

Doctors and nurses await the condemned. Medical equipment is there to administer the drugs. Everyone is highly trained. The room often functions as a perfected machine. Officials assure us that the procedure is painless. Once the drugs are administered, we're assured, "The offender safely falls asleep." How can anything be "safe" when the end result is death? There is nothing safe about our bloodlust. There is only our yearning for blood. There is only death. I couldn't believe they were doing this shit during Holy Week. Then again, I guess it fit the pattern.

"There is a fountain filled with blood drawn from Emmanuel's veins; and sinners plunged beneath that flood lose all their guilty stains."

We sang it over and over. As the organ played, fear kept creeping in. The night before, my cousin showed me one of the "A Nightmare on Elm Street" movies. Sweat dripped from my face. With every line, I grew more frightened. The preacher paused the music and declared, "God murdered his son to satisfy his wrath for your guilt. Blood is the only way out of here alive!" Scenes from the movie kept rushing back. God chased his son down a corridor. Knives extended from God's fingers. Reaching the corner, God slashed until his son was dead. Shouting out, I rushed to the front. I had to get out of the way of Freddy Krueger— or the God that murdered his own son. One of the pastors met me. Immediately, I prayed, "God, I'm a sinner. Don't take my blood! I trust in Jesus!" As tears streamed down my face, the pastor assured me that the blood was enough to protect me. I never believed him. If God was capable of murdering his own son, God was capable of anything.

True liberation only comes from the death of childish ideas. There once was a man named Paul. Before he met God, Paul believed that his mission in life was to run around killing folks. Paul believed that blood was the only path to what he wanted. Finally, God interrupted Paul's childish thinking with a dose of love. After he got saved, Paul wrote these words, "When the perfect comes, the partial is done away with. When I was a child, I spoke like a child, I understood as a child, I thought as a child; but when I grew up, I put away childish things." Only children deal in blood. Grownups deal in love.

Originating in our thirst for blood, the death penalty represents a failure to love. I don't think it's a coincidence that Christians often support the death penalty. Deadly theology leads to deadly practice. The death penalty is based on an idea that blood is required to atone for evil. We are carrying out an ancient ritual of atonement every time the state kills for us. The problem is that this denies any belief that Jesus is the atonement. God didn't kill Jesus. The love of Jesus is what took him to the cross. The atonement is love. How can we love and kill at the same time? We can't. Every time we carry out one of these executions we deny the love of Jesus. The death penalty has made us heretics. We are desperately in need of salvation.

Here in Texas, we are reenacting Holy Week. The difference is that Adam Ward is not Jesus. We are letting Ward say goodbye to his friends. We are giving Ward his final meal. We are leading Ward to the place. We are forcing Ward to climb up. We are making Ward extend his arms. We are piercing Ward's skin. We are murderers. There is no question that Ward murdered City of Commerce Code Enforcement Officer Michael "Pee Wee" Walker in 2005. There is also no question that we are about to do the same thing to him.

Blood doesn't help. Over and over, I put my faith in blood. No matter how many times I prayed, I got nowhere. The same is true of these executions. We can keep shedding blood all we want, but it won't get us anywhere. Our image of God must change. God is about restoration, not execution. We must let go of the fear before the love can pour in. God is here to save, not to kill. God is here to give power to blood. In the midst of the demand for blood, the power flows through sacrificing our blood for others. Jesus showed us that this is the greatest path. On this day, that path flows through Adam Ward.

"There is a fountain filled with blood drawn from Adam Ward's veins;
and sinners plunged beneath that flood lose all their guilty stains."

Dreams ran into each other. The result was the same. Jesus was standing in front of me. On one side was my body. On the other side was the easy life. The choice was mine. For many weeks, I struggled with the dream. I knew that Jesus was requiring more from me than he ever had. I realized I was being led to places I didn't anticipate going. Regardless, I refused the easy life. I wanted to follow Jesus. I knew where that path led. Amidst the evening rays of sun a few days before, I made the final decision to offer my body as a living sacrifice. I knew I wouldn't go alone.

Blood dripping down
All around our town
You are final-ly free
To come & get me

Executions

"It is finished." -John 19:30

Just like Pilate, many will try to absolve their responsibility for this premeditated murder. Instead of using a water basin, we just keep dehumanizing the condemned until we feel good about killing them. Loving your neighbor as your self doesn't work like that.

Our screams for blood and vengeance must be similar to the cries that Jesus heard before his execution. Our actions are similar too. We're carrying him to the execution chamber. We're strapping him to the gurney. We're injecting the poison. This is how evil people celebrate Holy Week. We reenact the execution.

I'm praying for some Holy Week conversions.

I'm praying we get saved from our addiction to executions.

I'm praying...

Put down the needle, Texas!

Walking home that night, I knew something wasn't right. Paranoia filled my brain. Panic filled my heart. Anxiety filled my stomach. Danger was everywhere. In the darkness, someone kept whispering my name. I begged them to stop. They laughed at me. No one was there. Closing my eyes, I raced down the sidewalk. Repeatedly, I felt people pulling and grabbing at me. Running full speed, I couldn't get to my dorm fast enough. When I opened the door, I saw evil incarnate in the form of the night guard. Feeling something in my pants, I knew I'd shit myself. Tears streamed down my face. "Get away from me!" I screamed. When I got to my room, I jumped in the bed. For hours, the demons tried to smother me. Waking up the next morning, I couldn't believe how destroyed my room was. I knew I did it. This wasn't the first time. Four years later, I was diagnosed with bipolar disorder.

Code enforcement in Commerce, Texas, received complaint after complaint concerning the home that Adam Ward shared with his dad. The department cited the Wards repeatedly. When Michael Walker arrived at the Ward home, there was no reason to believe that he would be doing anything other than performing the routine duties of a code enforcement officer. When Walker started taking pictures of violations, he didn't know that Adam Ward was suffering from delusions about the local government trying to kill him. Diagnosed with bipolar disorder when he was 4, Ward was spiraling. Ward began to argue with Walker. When Walker said that he was calling for back up, Ward's delusions told him that he was as good as dead. Running inside, Ward grabbed a gun. Without saying much, Ward ran at Walker and shot him nine times. Though Ward claimed that Walker had a gun too, there was never any evidence to prove it. The delusions haven't stopped. Ward was and is mentally ill.

Over the years, I've chosen not to own a gun. I've never felt healthy enough. I wish that Adam Ward had made the same choice. Maybe he was incapable of such decisions. Regardless, I know how quickly one can spiral out of control. I know what it looks like to be so paranoid and delusional that there is no way for you to be responsible for your actions. Ward is crazy like me. We are sick. There is no cure for our disease. While I have found a regiment of medicine that works pretty good for me, I know that the pills can only do so much. There are times when reality seems difficult to grasp. I don't know where Ward was with treatment. I only know that he was very sick. In Matthew 25, Jesus says that he is with the sick. Tonight, the State of Texas will try to execute Adam Ward. I know that Jesus will be there with him in his sickness. Jesus is always placing his body between the sick and those who seek their demise. We should too.

Throughout the day, I will travel to the execution chamber in Huntsville. Instead of commemorating Holy Week in a place of worship, I've chosen to experience the passion of Jesus in Adam Ward. When the State of Texas places the lethal needle into Ward's arm, I will be standing outside in defiance. We all know that Ward's actions aren't any crazier than the execution we are planning tonight. We think we can teach people not to kill by killing. Who's more delusional: Ward or us?

Finger after finger shook. I'd never seen fingers move like that. I tried to grab them. The shakes hit my hands. I clenched my fists. Then, the shakes traveled up my arms. I wondered what was going on. Before long, my entire body was shaking. I didn't know what to do. I needed strength. I didn't think I had it. Though the robe and stole concealed everything that was going on, I knew I wasn't well. "God, how am I going to do this?" Though people kept coming up to me to talk, I wasn't listening much. I couldn't. I just kept thinking. Adam Ward visited me in those moments. I was overwhelmed. I thought I was going to collapse. Everything was too much. I was coming apart. Then, *something* pulled me back together. Sacramental ideas started flowing through my mind. I could see the cup poured out. I could see the bread broken. Drawing me nearer, I could feel the presence of God. "I'm ready." The weather seemed to get slightly clearer. Everything seemed to move out of the way. My brain focused. I thought about all of the people who had been executed in that space. I could see so many faces. I could hear so many voices. I could feel their presence. I prayed. In those moments, I was with God. Looking down at the prison, I knew what I had to do.

Despite my fear
Jesus be near
Oh, despite my fear
Jesus be near

Every step felt like an eternity. Life was happening in slow motion. I didn't know if I'd ever get there. I never prepared for the struggle of it all. I thought I'd just be able to march down there and do it. It wasn't that simple. There was so much more to think about than just the placement of my feet. There were so many people who wanted to talk. Though I wasn't quite sure of what I was saying, I kept talking. I figured it was better to keep talking than actually to deal with my anxiety. The shakes were back. After the clock struck 6, I saw Ward again. God was there too. I lowered my head and started walking. Step by step, I moved toward the line. Though I'd seen that police line at every execution, I knew that it wouldn't hold me back this time. After I committed that final time, there was never a thought of turning back. This was Holy Week. This was a sacrament. This was the path of Jesus. "I will not turn back." The executed joined me for those final steps. Even though I walked alone, I could hear their footsteps. I think I even heard one of them say, "I am with you always, even to the end of the age." The officers seemed to have no idea what was going on. As I approached the police line, I said, "I'm coming across." Thoughts of Ward being executed rushed back into my brain. The nearest officer shouted, "No you're not!" I could've turned around during those seconds. I could've just decided that I'd done enough. I didn't.

It wasn't long before two officers were directly in front of me. Immediately, the officers tried to convince me to turn back. I didn't. I just kept praying. I hadn't made it this far to turn around. I knew God was with me. I pressed on. Both of the officers tried to convince me to turn back. I looked up and replied, "I can't do that." By this point, I could feel the presence of the executed standing around me. I knew they'd never left. We were all standing there together demanding an end to executions. God was with us. When the officer said that he was going to take me to jail, I knew I wasn't going alone. As I was placed under arrest and walked to the car, I looked up. The sun gleamed off the cross atop the prison. "That shit is fake." I knew that the real cross was out here with us. As we drove off into the sunset, I felt God whisper, "Well done."

As soon as I got to the jail, I was processed like any other criminal. There were few people there that night. Before I knew it, I was alone. There behind the bars, I started to pray. Once again, Adam Ward visited me. I prayed for those who killed him. I knew that I was one of them. The prayers started to propel my feet around the cell. God gave me visions of all that had transpired. The passion continued. *The steps.* Pilgrimage propelled me to that line. *The encounters.* Relationships with the condemned pushed me over that line. *The anger.* Defiance granted me the courage to refuse to move back over that line. Everything I'd known in my work for abolition culminated in my sacramental act of civil disobedience in front of the prison that night. The cell felt like a place of completion. I was able to rest with God and the executed. I saw their faces. The darkness wouldn't last much longer. Late that night, I made bail. I hurried to the car and left. When the rising rays of sun met the clouds, I was on the road thinking about the killing of the condemned. Though the night had been long, I knew that that all of the bullshit would soon be over. Executions can't live forever.

Time was no more.

Behold, I saw God die. I wept. I didn't know what to do. After they placed the sheet over the body, I turned away. I just wanted to get out of there. Not long after I turned back, I saw the sheet start to rise. God was alive! Death was no more. In a fit of rage, God destroyed the gurney. The damn thing exploded into a million pieces. I heard God say loudly, "It is finished."

BENEDICTION

Now, may the God who learned to stop killing be the God who keeps you from killing.

Amen.